Praise for
You're Embarrassing Yourself

"Desiree Akhavan's memoir is a hilariously raw, relatable, and—dare I even say—sexy recounting of an awkward girl's journey to finding her way as an adult and, ultimately, an artist. . . . In other words—a perfect book."

—JESSI KLEIN, *New York Times* bestselling author of *I'll Show Myself Out*

"Addictively honest and cool without leaving anyone out, this book offers a hand and a laugh to readers who have gone through some of the same things that Desiree Akhavan did— which, let's be honest, is most of us. Clearly I'm embarrassing myself because after reading her book I want so desperately to be best friends with Akhavan. And you will too!"

—CASEY WILSON, *New York Times* bestselling author of *The Wreckage of My Presence*

"An utterly charming, hilarious coming-of-art story, full to the brim with cringe and heart."

—MELISSA FEBOS, nationally bestselling author of *Body Work* and *Girlhood*

"Full of heart, thrumming with profundity, and laugh-out-loud hilarious, *You're Embarrassing Yourself* marks Desiree Akhavan as a blazing literary talent. Come for the gossip and cringe; stay for the moving portraits of familial loyalty, queerness, art making, and the many ways we find ourselves home. I toted this book around with me like it was my best friend, and that's what Akhavan feels like as the book's narrator: candid, clever, shining with the promise that anything is possible. In this memoir—it is."

—T KIRA MADDEN, author of
Long Live the Tribe of Fatherless Girls

"With cackle-worthy humor and absolute ease, Desiree Akhavan shares her deeply honest stories of culture and identity, modern sexuality, and what it is to be an artist. I laughed, I cried, and then I laughed again."

—LENA DUNHAM, #1 *New York Times* bestselling
author of *Not That Kind of Girl*

"Each of these essays feels like a satisfying night out with your most funny, sexy, and self-deprecating friend. Together they add up to a moving account of self-acceptance that gives us each permission to take it all a little less seriously."

—ANNA SALE, host of the podcast *Death, Sex & Money*
and author of *Let's Talk About Hard Things*

You're Embarrassing Yourself

You're Embarrassing Yourself

Stories of Love, Lust, and Movies

Desiree Akhavan

RANDOM HOUSE

New York

A Random House Trade Paperback Original

Copyright © 2024 by Desiree Akhavan

Published in the United States by Random House,
an imprint and division of Penguin Random House LLC, New York.

RANDOM HOUSE and the HOUSE colophon are registered
trademarks of Penguin Random House LLC.

ISBN 978-0-399-58850-1
Ebook ISBN 978-0-399-58849-5

Printed in the United States of America on acid-free paper

randomhousebooks.com

2 4 6 8 9 7 5 3 1

FIRST EDITION

Book design by Mary A. Wirth

For Yasmin, Cyrous, and Ardavan

Contents

Introduction

OR

How Did I Get Like This?

There was a time before shame.

A time of Pogs, Tamagotchis, and the Macarena. When birthday party invites were a given, books came with charm necklaces, and whoever was in your class was automatically a friend. Our moms would handle the admin of our social lives, and every so often I'd find myself in an exotic living room, staging a music video to something off *Jagged Little Pill*, and it 100 percent did not matter that there was no camera to record it, because dancing with scarves while lip-synching to Alanis Morissette for an audience of your friend's little brother was the pinnacle of the creative process. This was back when we were smart enough to know that art was meant to be created and then immediately forgotten, like an Etch A Sketch or the hundreds of origami paper cranes a music teacher insisted we fold for some altruistic reason I never quite grasped. These were the golden years of girlhood. Then puberty hit, *Clueless* came out, and everything got shitty.

Suddenly pens needed feather tails or they were for losers.

It was 1995. Earlier that year, the O. J. Simpson trial steam-rolled over my summer soap opera viewing schedule of *All My Children* at one, followed by *One Life to Live* at two. Every day I'd cross all my fingers and silently pray that ABC would re-sume its regularly scheduled programming, and every day the trial dragged on with no end in sight. I should have known my whole world was about to turn sinister.

The weekend before the first day of fifth grade, Jessica King invited me over for a slumber party. We were about to be in the same class, but we'd never met before. I had no idea why she chose to invite me, but I knew she was popular and that it was an honor. Yet I didn't even labor over the decision: I im-mediately told my mom to decline because the sleepover was the same night I was scheduled to perform "Hot Cross Buns" on the recorder with my theater day camp at the Tappan Zee High School auditorium, and it was a commitment I took way too seriously.

How could I have known the decision to choose "Hot Cross Buns" over that sleepover would be fatal? I thought life would be full of unsolicited slumber party invites. I still wonder what kind of person I'd have become if I'd chosen differently. To be fair, there's a pretty good chance they would've gotten a whiff of my penchant for Tracey Ullman–style impressions and hated me anyway, but what if they *hadn't*? What if I'd gone and they'd found my various accents "quirky" and endearing in the vein of Kate Winslet's potato people figurines in *Eternal Sun-shine*? What if I'd gone and it cemented my place among what was about to become *The* Most Popular Clique at School? That sleepover was where they formed their union. With Jessica King as their leader, that group of eleven-year-old girls be-came the definition of cool. If I'd been accepted as one of them from the start, it would have changed fifth grade. Sixth grade too. Maybe even my whole life?

But I didn't go. I chose "Hot Cross Buns."

That year, The Most Popular Clique at School started playing *Clueless* as a recess game. How do you play the Paramount Pictures smash hit and cultural phenomenon *Clueless* as a recess game? I have no idea, because when I asked if I could join in, I was told that I would need to interview, which struck me as strange since even Min-ji Shin, the new girl who'd just arrived in America and didn't speak English, was given the role of Summer, no questions asked. But I kept my mouth shut and scheduled an interview.

The next morning, I pulled my hair up into a high ponytail and brought down two long wisps at the front (which I decided would henceforth be my "signature look"). I borrowed my mom's Ann Taylor sleeveless turtleneck, paired it with a plaid miniskirt, and thought, *Damn, girl, well played*, when I saw my reflection in the school bus window. For the interview, I sat before a tribunal of Jessica and her posse as they addressed me with an air of authority only a group of yellow-haired white girls with trust funds could muster at the age of eleven, and by the time recess was over I was confident I'd nailed it. I floated through the rest of the afternoon with the smug self-satisfaction of a girl with recess plans locked down for the rest of the year.

I was waiting to board the bus home when I was informed that my application for Clueless: The Recess Game had been denied. Again, I saw my reflection in the bus window. The wisps of hair framing my face looked stringy and stupid. Who was I fooling in my too-tight plaid miniskirt that I'd had to hold my breath in to button? I was ten going on eleven and already my mom's clothes were too small. I hadn't felt self-conscious about it up until that moment.

That was the day my pace slowed and everyone else's progressed. As we got older and my classmates threw parties and developed Adderall dependencies, I spent the majority of my time alone, watching TV and giving pretend E! interviews about my life as the latest cast member of *Dawson's Creek* (and Joshua Jackson's girlfriend).

That year marked the origin of my shame. It was when I became cognizant of my hooked Iranian nose, my towering height, and the folds of flesh jutting out over my waistband. It was also the year I wrote my first script: a comedy sketch show called *Friday Night Live* that featured an ad for a product called "Vomlet: The Omelet Made of Vomit!"

When I pitched the idea for this book, I was having a moment. I'd just released my first film, *Appropriate Behavior*, and when it premiered, I received more attention and praise than I'd thought possible for a girl like me. This led me to believe that life was split between two phases: an ugly duckling period, followed by a swan rest-of-your-life. I assumed that everything I'd faced up until that point had been the price of admission, and that I was finally the swan I'd always hoped lay dormant beneath my old nose and about forty pounds of baby fat. I decided to write a book that could serve as a guide for misfits: I overcame the worst things that happened to me, and so can you! But then swan life soured, and I still had this book to write on how I'd "made it."

They say, "You'll grow out of it," but you might not. Yes, you'll eventually grow into something new, maybe even something spectacular, but if you're anything like me, you'll always clutch the moniker "loser" close to your heart. At first it'll feel like a handicap, but eventually it'll transform into a superpower, because being on the outside offers up the best vantage point from which to observe and skewer. Now, almost a decade after I began writing this book, I see it as an artifact of who I was and who I became from nineteen to thirty-nine, as I inched my way into adulthood by making every mistake possible.

Seventeen magazine had a column called "Traumarama" that brought me a lot of joy in the '90s. Girls wrote in their most embarrassing stories anonymously: "The boy I have a crush on mistook my tampon string for a loose thread on my swimsuit and pulled it out at a pool party!" "I was home alone, out of clean clothes, and heading to the laundry machine naked when I ran into my dad and three of his co-workers!" During my teens, that column was the only thing I could relate to. Sometimes it feels as if my years on earth have been a compilation of one Traumarama after another: humiliating, a bit disgusting, and actually pretty funny if you take a step back.

These essays are my ode to Traumarama; they recount the most cringe-inducing moments of my life—the ones that formed me. I wrote it for the ugly, the unfuckable, the horny, the insatiable, the foreign, the misfits, the rejects, the outcasts, and the losers. The ones who talk too much, want too much, love too hard and too fast. Who lay all their cards on the table. Who eat their feelings or fuck their feelings, or eat *and* fuck their feelings until they're good and spent. Who lived their youths dripping with shame but never allowed that shame to silence them. Here are the stories of how I became a beast, a cutter, a bulimic, a homo, a filmmaker, a slut, an egomaniac, a woman.

You're
Embarrassing
Yourself

What I Wish
I'd Known at Ten

- After the age of twenty-five nobody will ever ask where you went to college.
- One day Mimi Wright will wear the short-sleeve black-and-white-striped mock-neck bodysuit, jeans, and hoodie you both saw and appreciated on the mannequin at The Limited. Do not give in to the temptation to wear that exact same outfit to school the very next day. It will *not* bond the two of you so that from now on you'll coordinate outfits like twins, and it *will* result in her never speaking to you again.
- One day, not as soon, Laura Stark will orchestrate it so that all the girls start coughing as soon as you sit to eat lunch with them. They will cough and cough until you get the hint and leave. This will be no great loss. I repeat, NO GREAT LOSS.
- Your face and shape will shift and morph and sometimes scare you, but eventually settle into something you'll be able to live with by the time you turn thirty.

- Forget about that article you read in *JUMP* magazine about the girl in Missouri who, at seventeen, went from flat to double D's overnight. These are your tits for life.

The Beast

Remember HotorNot.com? It was one of the most highly trafficked websites of the early aughts. The name pretty much says it all. People uploaded photos of themselves, and users would vote: hot or not. Back then, we had a huge Dell desktop that lived in my brother Ardavan's room, and before I could even touch it I'd have to hassle my mom to get off the phone to free up the line. Then came the process of logging on to the internet, which had a soundscape that, to this day, elicits a Pavlovian response of making my heart race in anticipation. At the time, the very existence of the internet was surreal and a bit exhilarating. I chose to use my first precious hours with it doomscrolling HotorNot. I was there to train my eye, and as I did a pattern emerged: skinny symmetrical white girls in bikinis = hot, the rest of us = not.

When I was fourteen, someone created a website where you could vote for the hottest girl at my school. I went to an elite New York City private school that took itself so seriously that when you were asked where you went to school, you'd watch yourself stiffen with a pseudo-humble *Maybe you've heard of it?* People in New York knew about Horace Mann. It was both famous and infamous, and I couldn't decide if I should be proud or horrified.

To explain why Horace Mann was what it was, I need to set the scene. New York City sells itself as a haven for weirdos: inclusive and radical. It's not. You have to be a certain kind of hot, rich, and successful to play—the rest of us are just extras. It's a city built on hierarchies with a small town's penchant for gossip. People make the pilgrimage to New York because they believe, deep in their bones, that they might be the very best at something. In turn, the city remains in a constant state of flux, perpetually measuring exactly who and what is "the best." There's always a *best* neighborhood, a *best* handbag, a *best* restaurant, a *best* play, and so of course the schools were measured up against one another and it was agreed by many that Horace Mann was the *best* of the *best*. Or at least that's what our parents told themselves to justify the exorbitant tuition fees.

The students didn't just live on Park Avenue; they lived in penthouses on Park Avenue, where the elevator doors open up into the living room. Many parents fell into the category of "New York famous," which means profiled in the *Times*, but nobody outside the Citarella delivery zone has ever heard of you. Renée Fleming famous. It was shockingly overpriced, shockingly elite, shocking for about forty-seven other reasons, like the molestation of teen boys by an Austrian choir conductor who'd strut through the halls like he was Mick Jagger.

My parents put every cent they had into sending my brother and me to the best. They even took out a third mortgage on their house to make it happen. Having moved to America from Iran not knowing much about the country, the people, or the rules, they were confident that the strongest advantage they could offer was to send us to the same school as the children of the richest and most powerful, so we could mingle with them and then morph into exemplary American versions of ourselves. It's a strategy that worked for my brother, Ardavan, who was academically gifted and disciplined. I don't know if he mingled with the spawn of the New York elite socially, but he definitely excelled among them and adopted a sense of rigid perfection that continues to elude me. From Horace Mann he went on to Columbia University, then the University of Pittsburgh School of Medicine, and is currently one of the country's leading pediatric urological surgeons.

I was never sure if I'd be able to return on that investment. For me, unlike my brother, Horace Mann didn't make sense. It was a place for future investment bankers, doctors, lawyers, politicians, and trophy wives. Your currency lay in being the richest, the smartest, and (duh) the hottest, which of course is true of every school, but we were all high off our own farts, so of course we would go and make our own version of HotorNot.

I say "we," but I shouldn't. It wasn't just that I didn't belong. "Not belonging" is too passive. You can not belong and still function in a place. I was a different species from the rest of them. At fourteen, I had exactly one friend: Nina Klein, a high-strung, straight-A parent pleaser and competitive gymnast who taught me that grapes have ten calories apiece. Every day we'd eat lunch in the girls' locker room so we'd be early for gym. You know, the way cool kids do.

I knew I wouldn't be on the Hottest Girls at Horace Mann website, but that didn't stop me from checking it every time I was within twenty feet of a computer. Knowing you're not part of the conversation doesn't stop you from wanting to eavesdrop and then mold yourself in the image of those who are, obsessing over every detail of their face, body, and wardrobe, scanning to see what you can copy in the hope of dragging yourself a little closer to the heart of it. I felt compelled to track who was winning the Hottest Girls at Horace Mann as if it were the presidential primary.

One day I got an email from an address I didn't recognize. Inside was a link and nothing else. The link led me to a site with the header "The Ugliest Girls at Horace Mann." The layout was exactly like its sister site, only next to the names were adorable nicknames like "the Slut," "the Bitch," "Butterface." Most of the girls listed were actually pretty popular and conventionally hot, so I got the sense the site was an inside joke made to settle a vendetta. But then I saw my own name. Next to it, "the Beast."

I knew I was going to be on that site the minute I saw "Ugliest." I knew it instinctively, the way I knew liver would taste mealy, like an overripe tomato, before it ever touched my tongue. My name earned a whopping forty-two votes, while the others had two or three each. There's no way the creators had a vendetta to settle with me. Eating lunch alone with Nina Klein in the girls' locker room meant sidestepping vendettas. It was undeniable: I was the only person on the list who'd made it there because she was legitimately ugly. Not a bitch; a beast.

You know when something *bad* happens, worse than your worst nightmare, and the pure drama of it fills you with a weird sense of satisfaction? Satisfaction laced in endorphins. There was something almost euphoric about the sheer intensity of seeing my name on that website.

I felt starstruck, knowing I was watching a seminal life moment take shape before my eyes, as I refreshed the page every thirty seconds to watch my votes go up. Starstruck plus nostalgic for the life I'd been living an hour earlier, before I'd gotten the email. I'd always had a suspicion, but now I had empirical proof: I was the Ugliest.

I'd started to get the sense I might be ugly around eleven, when adults began offering up unsolicited hair, diet, exercise, and plastic surgery advice. It was about that time that I learned what "hot" was, and how it seemed to be the price of admission if you were a girl. Any woman who didn't classify as hot was automatically relegated to being the butt of the joke. Or at least that's what I'd gleaned from Howard Stern, who spoke on the matter for ninety minutes straight each morning, blasting through the bus speakers on the way to school.

But it wasn't just Howard; it's in my blood. Iranians are spectacularly superficial. Presentation is everything. We sub-scribe to a "more is more" aesthetic: full face of makeup to go to the grocery store. We're serving baroque, air-kisses on both cheeks, grass-is-greener-on-my-side realness. You can't drive home from a party without going through a full breakdown of who got fat and who got old, like Mom and Dad are Joan Riv-ers's Fashion Police and you're their backseat studio audience.

Should I just go ahead and blame my mom? Sure, why not? She's naturally thin and small boned with a tiny waist and big eyes, and I don't look anything like her. Actually, that's not true: I inherited her flat chest. Growing up, people felt com-pelled to tell me how beautiful she was with a mixture of awe and shock, as if her hotness was a party trick I'd managed to pull off. Then they'd follow up with "You know you look *exactly* like your dad?" They're right. I'm a carbon copy: thick in the middle with a long forehead and feet so big I have to ask if they carry size 11 before I fully enter the store. The fat that should have gone to my tits and my ass accumulated in my stomach, which has been the focus of 80 percent of all my brain activity since 1996.

Nobody said a word about the site at school the next day, but from the moment I was crowned the Beast, my whole world shifted. Every room transformed into a hierarchy of hotness. They say beauty's only skin-deep, as if what doesn't make it to your face and ass gets redirected to your heart, but

I sometimes wonder if it's not the ugly who have the cruelest takedowns of their own ugliness (plus everyone else's). Becoming the Beast made me superficial. Decades passed, and even though I eventually grew into my forehead, lost weight, and did two stints of Accutane, I still couldn't pass a reflective surface without stealing a glance to catch what was staring back: woman or beast?

I developed a permanent suspicion that the way I looked was fucking me over and that I was operating at a deficit from the moment I entered a room. I was the Beast for so long that even once I crawled my way to something different, I couldn't decide *what* I'd become without looking to strangers for answers.

I'd do it late at night. In my most pathetic hours.

When I was drunk or sleepy.

When even though I knew the rule of being a functional human is NO SCREENS IN THE BEDROOM, I went ahead and turned one into my pacifier.

When I'd gone down a clickbait spiral of YouTube clips from "Plus Size Bride Finds Dress of Her Dreams" to "5 Spices That Healed My Gut" to "Low Cost Scandinavia Inspired Tiny House Tour," each video hitting like empty calories that go straight from your eyes to your subconscious without even tasting.

When I knew that if I couldn't sleep, I should be reading or journaling or yin-yoga-ing, but I'd have rather gnawed my arm off than pressed play on the guided meditation app my three most aspirational friends called "life changing."

When it felt like my brain had been scooped out until I was all rind, no melon—

That was when I would google myself.

Some of the photos were the ideal version of me: well-lit and just the right angle, eye contact, and subtle smile that comes more from the heart than the teeth. Others were like looking into a funhouse mirror, like the time a heavy-handed makeup artist convinced me we were channeling Bowie, or when a botched bob made me look like an ambiguously ethnic Shirley Temple. In some photos, I looked straight-up deranged, like a series from the hospitality lounge at the Indie Spirit Awards, where I felt so bad for the intern tasked with asking celebrities to pose for Breyers ice cream that I agreed to be photographed presenting a gallon of rocky road in an evening gown like an off-brand *Deal or No Deal* girl.

When you're cobbling together a sense of identity through your Google search results, the praise, love, and accolades slide right off like eggs on Teflon, but when you find the criticism, it's like a stranger's homed in on the truth of you. Or at least that's how it felt when I found a long thread on my IMDb profile, back when each one had its own message board, debating whether or not I was born male.

Being mistaken for trans wasn't the insult; it was the masculinity they pinpointed that scared the shit out of me. "She looks like a man to me too," I read over and over.

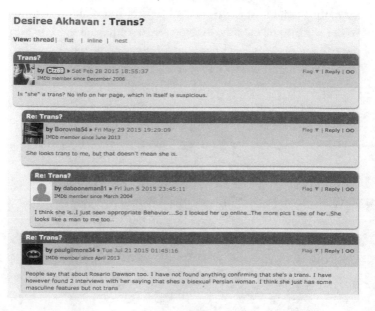

They're not wrong. I'm not particularly feminine: I have big hands, the kind of hands you can't find gloves for in the women's department. Big hands, big feet, and a strong jaw, broad shoulders, flat chest, and no delicate features whatsoever. What's strange is that when I made the film that prompted those IMDb comments, my perspective on all those features shifted. Making work I was proud of transformed me into someone I liked the look of. I didn't need to be delicate or feminine to be a great leader. In fact, my big hands, big feet, strong jaw, and broad shoulders lent me an air of authority. I looked like a leader. And, for the first time in my life, I felt genuinely beautiful. But the feeling slipped through my fingers during the press and photos and reviews that followed the making of that film. It was like I'd put myself up on HotorNot for anyone to judge.

Fortunately, there's a real joy to aging while gay. It's made me realize that Howard Stern and HotorNot and all those other voices rattling around my thirteen-year-old brain were irrelevant. They made it seem like the only way to be a woman who had power and fun was to be Pam Anderson in the '90s. But how could that be true if the moments when I'm at my greatest are when I'm in my Carhartts, staring into a monitor with no eyes on me at all? The tragedy isn't that I was the Ugliest Girl at Horace Mann, but that I never saw the site for what it was: a group of teen boys desperately trying to pull focus from their own mediocrity.

The HotorNot definition of beauty is a construct that's constantly shifting. I know this because I've watched it morph from a pencil-thin Kate Moss to an athletic Gabrielle Reece, to a slim thick Kim Kardashian, to whatever it'll become now that everyone's having their butt and hip implants removed. And even though I know all this, and say all this, and believe it to be true, the truth *beneath* that truth is that being voted the Ugliest Girl at Horace Mann shaped me and everything that was to come. I took the title and ran with it, repeating it to myself like a mantra: I am the ugliest. The Ugliest. *The* Ugliest.

I don't google myself late at night looking for answers anymore. There are no answers to be found in the hands of strangers on the internet. I can continue to tell myself the story of who I am through the eyes of high school bullies, or I can allow myself the simple pleasure of having my own opinion. I'm not for everyone, but perhaps nobody should be for everyone. I am the Beast: tall and thick and loud and strong and hungry and a little bit hairy. What a waste that I allowed myself to believe that was anything short of a gift.

A Cokehead I Met in a
Support Group
for Cutters

I was the ten-year-old who felt more comfortable chilling with your mom in the kitchen while she frosted cake than at the actual birthday party. I'd ask invasive questions about her childhood and the career aspirations that were put on hold when she got pregnant. In return, I got a lot of "So mature for your age!" and "You're really going to come into your own at college." I got through my teens by fantasizing about college, where I imagined the social hierarchy would flip like in my favorite episode of *The Twilight Zone*, where people with horrifying melted pig faces are considered hot and a beautiful Grace Kelly type is treated like a leper.

I ended up at a small women's liberal arts school in western Massachusetts for the same reason I went to prom with a friend of a friend's drug dealer who fell into a k-hole about an hour into the night: it was my only option. I'd applied to thirteen schools and gotten rejected by most of them. The small women's liberal arts school said yes, so I said yes, but it wasn't a great fit, and from the first few hours of orientation, it became clear to me that most girls there fell into one of three categories: pearl-wearing legacy princess, queer hipster, or that quiet girl who used to knit in the back of your high school English class.

The pearl-wearing legacy princess came from a blue-blood American family, where her mother, grandmother, and aunties had all attended the same small women's liberal arts school. She'd definitely vote Republican in five years, but for the moment she was experimenting with liberalism (but not lesbianism). She was never seen without the Elsa Peretti for Tiffany open-heart necklace her father had given her on her sixteenth birthday, she woke up at 6 A.M. to blow out her hair, and she only partied at Amherst, where she'd eventually meet her husband.

The queer hipsters bowed down to the same exclusionary hierarchies that existed in high school, only instead of the blond trust fund cheerleader at the peak of the social ladder, it was the gender-queer top with a mullet, gauged ears, and a sleeve of stick 'n' poke tattoos.

Meanwhile, the painfully shy girl who used to knit in the back of your high school English class wouldn't leave her dorm's common room for the entirety of freshman year and said so little in class you couldn't tell if she was the best or the worst student there (but you were confident it was one or the other). There was a 35 percent chance she'd lose her virginity to her roommate, then come out as asexual when she'd break off their engagement six years later.

And that's it. Those were the types of girls it felt like you could be.

I tried to fit in, sharing the tiniest edge of blanket with a group of painfully earnest Christians while watching *28 Days Later* in the common room on a Saturday night, all of us decked out in the kind of loungewear your mom insists on buying during that mind-melting precollege trip to Bed Bath & Beyond (baby-blue terry cloth robe covered in smiling clouds). I tried to fit in, squeezing into too-tight lowrider jeans and my biggest hoop earrings to tag along with my much cooler roommate (who was very kind to invite me) and her JLo wannabe friends (who were less kind) when we went barhopping in town. I tried to fit in, wearing a padded suit and paper wig playing Virgil Thomson in a spoken-word operetta about the life and times of Susan B. Anthony. I tried, but failed, and the trying left me emptier than if I hadn't tried at all.

It snowed during first-trimester finals. Late one night, I heard squeals outside my window and looked out to see a swarm of girls running naked through the snow. I knew that if I didn't go downstairs, take my clothes off, and streak through the quad squealing with delight, I wouldn't be partaking in "the College Experience." I also knew that if I *did* join in, I'd be late and uninvited. The clock was ticking. I didn't know how much longer they'd be out there. I rationalized that maybe the key to fitting in was to fake it till I made it. In the movies, isn't bravery always rewarded? In *Rudy*, the tiniest, shittiest football player at Notre Dame is finally allowed to play in the game, then carried off the field on the shoulders of his teammates like a goddamned hero. I rationalized that trying always beats not trying, and that I, like Rudy, would find my place at college if I just kept at it. So I went outside, took my clothes off, and did an impression of wholesome college girl fun.

I ran a full naked lap around the quad, while everything inside me screamed, *WHY THE FUCK ARE YOU DOING THIS?* I smiled and I laughed and I even forced out a "WOOOOOOOOHOOOOOOOO!" as I watched people form lifelong bonds from about ten feet behind. And afterward, as I watched my housemates towel off, rosy-cheeked and glowing, I felt more alone than I'd ever felt in my entire life. It was the kind of loneliness that takes your breath away—my chest ached with it. I couldn't relate to a single person, nor could anybody relate to me. Not just at school, but anywhere I went.

It was around that time that I started cutting. I'd been experimenting with various forms of self-harm and had heard good things. I wanted to *look* as weak and pathetic as I *felt* (think 1993 Kate Moss), but my body was undermining me. Cutting seemed like an effective way to cultivate the "damsel in distress" persona I'd been coveting since a friend's Eastern European grandmother described my body as "built for manual labor." I wanted to transform the way I felt into a tangible physical *thing* that could congeal and scab and scar and exist outside my heart and my head. Unfortunately, cutting didn't provide the emotional catharsis I was after, but that didn't stop me from becoming attached to the ritual of it. Eventually, I turned myself in to a counselor at the school health care center, who referred me to an on-campus support group for self-harm, and I was HERE FOR IT. A place that would reinforce my sense of victimization *and* introduce me to new people? Yes, please! My new friends and I would connect over how DEEP and TORTURED we were, bound together by our shameful secret! I silently patted myself on the back for choosing a vice that justified its very own category of group therapy.

Unfortunately, the support group for cutters wasn't the fun-time social hour I thought it would be. It turns out most cutters *aren't* super interested in translating their pain into words before an audience of peers as if they're doing sense memory work at a Meisner class and are more interested in playing the silent game while staring down at their feet. What our group therapy lacked in confessional monologues it made up for in handouts that listed alternatives for cutting like "Take a shower" or "Eat hot peppers until your nose runs." But it all fell on deaf ears, because the minute I entered the first meeting, I came face-to-face with the hottest girl I'd ever seen in real life, and from that moment on, Monday afternoons from four to five thirty became less about recovery and more about carving the memory of every last detail of her face and body into my mind.

Her name was Nisha, and she was an international student from India. Her hair was hacked into a DIY pixie, poorly bleached, and dyed cotton candy blue. She was long and lanky with perfect tits, and since she always looked bored and spoke so infrequently, I was sure she was thinking something brilliant that would have gone way over my head. I gushed about her constantly to my a cappella group but never made a move.

Did I forget to mention I was in an a cappella group? We were called the Noteables, and I had solos in our renditions of "I Put a Spell on You" and "Take on Me." Perhaps you heard these tracks on *The New Pink*, the CD we recorded with money we earned singing in front of people who went along with it because, like improv comedy and ultimate Frisbee, a cappella is just one of those things you have to pretend to enjoy while attending a liberal arts school. The fact that I'd not only started cutting but also joined an a cappella group at college is a real testament to how desperate I'd become.

I genuinely dislike the sound of voices singing with no musical accompaniment, not to mention the fact that when you're in an a cappella group, giving a good performance means bouncing up and down while making DIRECT EYE CONTACT with the other members as you sing. But the absolute worst part of being in an a cappella group was that every so often a male group would come to do a guest set at one of our concerts, then stick around to party, at which point all the straight girls would compete for attention until the one who felt least loved by her father wound up crouched in a communal bathroom with a dick in her mouth. All that said, the Noteables were the most kind and supportive people I encountered at the small women's liberal arts school. They were my only friends that first year of college and I'll always be grateful. They're also the reason I lost my virginity.

It turned out that Grace, a petite second alto who stands out in my mind as having confessed to masturbating with vegetables during a game of Truth or Dare,* lived in the same house as Nisha, my obsession from the support group for cutters. I'd sworn everyone in the Noteables to secrecy, but Grace, understanding that the codes of slumber party secrecy are flexible when crushes are involved, went rogue. A week later I got a call on my dorm room phone.

"Hello?"

The silence lasted long enough that I was about to hang up when I heard, ". . . Is this Desiree?"

"Yes."

"Um. What's up?"

"May I ask who's calling?"

Have you ever uttered a phrase on autopilot and then thought, *Mom? Did you just speak through me like a ventriloquist?*

"It's Nisha."

My heart bounced up to my esophagus, then down to the pit of my stomach, then back up again, where it remained for the next six months. I had no idea she even knew my name.

"Oh. Hey."

"Hey."

"What's up?"

"Nothing."

---

* Once a semester the Noteables would orchestrate a night of "Note-a-bonding," which meant getting drunk on wine coolers and playing sleepover games that culminated in a disgustingly chaste round of Spin the Bottle.

"Cool."

We'd continue to bat witty repartee like that for the entirety of our relationship.

"Wanna come over for, like, tea or something?"

"To your dorm?"

"Yeah."

"Okay."

And then she hung up.

An hour later we were sitting on her bed. I had one goal on my mind, and that was to make sure the evening became sexual. Neither of us had said a word for a solid five minutes. She put on music. I would soon learn that she played the same 8-track playlist of R&B songs from 1997 on loop. Janet Jackson's "Every Time" was the soundtrack to our love. The room was sparse and a bit depressing, which struck me as strange. I'd assumed beautiful people automatically knew how to curate beautiful spaces: that somehow everything she touched would morph to match her. Perhaps that was another reason I was so desperate for her to touch me.

"Do you wanna smoke?"

"Okay."

I expected her to whip out the pack of rainbow Nat Shermans I'd seen her lighting on the way out of group therapy, but instead she went for a small drawer in her nightstand. She arranged her pot-smoking accoutrements between us on the bed: a glass pipe, a grinder, an Altoid tin filled with weed, and an empty toilet paper roll stuffed with dryer sheets to blow the smoke out of (which I assumed she'd single-handedly invented but came to learn was a staple in every college dorm room in North America). Watching her pack the bowl was like watching a striptease; each move made me more aware of my skin and the air around it. Even my knees felt horny. She had an air about her that said she didn't give a shit. She could take it or leave it. Anything—me, college, the weed. That kind of indifference struck me as mildly cruel, and incredibly sexy.

She stuffed a towel under the door. Fan on, window open, and the room filled with a thin film of dryer sheet–filtered smoke. I was aware that with each passing second I was inching closer to the moment I'd have to leave. I was jealous of myself at 6 P.M., when I'd first stepped through the door. I expected her to initiate the transition to sex stuff, but she didn't. I was at that stage of inexperience where the shift from hanging out to making out feels insurmountable. Someone needed to put it all out on the line, but I knew that one overzealous move would kill the vibe.

"When are you going to kiss me?"

The words escaped my lips, then hung in the air like a silent, potent fart. I had a habit sometimes of talking like I thought I was in a John Hughes film, and it was never as cute or endearing out loud as it played in my head. She didn't respond. I silently counted the seconds: *Three Mississippi. Four Mississippi. Five Missi* . . .

"Yeah, okay."

She said it like I'd invited her to my friend's kid's piano recital, but the next thing I knew we were kissing, and it was awesome.

In the last month of high school, a boy named Eli had licked my right nipple for a good three minutes during a party after *my* friend told *his* friend I thought he was cute. I remember apologizing for being flat chested, and Eli accepting my apology. This was different. With Eli the tit-licker, it was just skin on skin.

I want to accurately describe what it was like kissing Nisha, stoned, in her huge dorm room, which was supposed to be a double but which she got all to herself on account of all the mental and behavioral problems. It was magic. It was my first taste of mutual attraction. It was like dancing when your body and the bass line fall in sync and it feels like you're being held up and moved by a force greater than muscle and bone. It was like strapping into a roller-coaster—more specifically, a run-down, malfunctioning roller-coaster in rural Italy that hasn't been serviced since the 1950s.

We made out for about ten minutes before she realized she'd made plans with a friend and had to go. She said this, and then, instead of leaving, I OFFERED TO WAIT IN HER ROOM UNTIL SHE GOT BACK. What I still don't quite understand is why she agreed, after just ten minutes of second-time-in-my-life kissing. As soon as she was gone, I called my friend Wendy from the Noteables, said, "GUESS WHERE I'M CALLING YOU FROM?," and for the next two hours re-counted a play-by-play of what had just happened. Then Nisha returned, I hung up on Wendy, and we had sex to the same four Janet Jackson songs on repeat.

The thing about sex that I couldn't have known until it was happening was that my body had a dialogue with her body that didn't involve my brain in any way. For the first time it was my lust, not my insecurities, calling the shots, and I was shocked by how powerful that lust turned out to be. There was confidence and self-assurance in my hands and my tongue that had always eluded me. I shocked myself by knowing exactly what I wanted to do. The squeaky metal-frame bed, the repetitive music, the laundry-weed air—it was all completely intoxicating. Afterward, as the sun rose and Nisha snored, I wrapped myself in the duvet she'd kicked off the bed and stood out on her balcony, overlooking the botanical garden. It was the first best moment of my life. It was also the last best moment I shared with Nisha.

Here are some facts I came to learn about Nisha Devi in the weeks that followed: she'd stopped going to classes and was on the brink of failing out of school; she'd taken all the money her parents had given her for a computer, food, and books and spent it on cocaine; and she had the feeling something bad had happened to her on a recent trip to New York but was too fucked up to remember exactly what.

I was in over my head and had no idea how to help her, but I was also pretty sure she was the only person in the world who would ever want to see me naked, so I developed a "can do" attitude to her rehabilitation through sex and kindness. Nisha thought I was attractive and referred to me as "hot" on more than one occasion. What amazed me was that she did not value *any* of my other qualities. One time I came over with a crazy story about some drama I'd seen unfold in the campus center and she snapped, "Every time I see you, you say, 'The funniest thing just happened,' but the funniest thing can't keep happening to you every single time you leave the house!" I remember this moment so clearly because up until that point, my ability to find comedy in the banal was the only thing I sort of liked about myself. Nisha seemed to only want me for my looks, and that made me feel FANTASTIC. Objectifying a girl whose defining feature had always been her "great personality" is the most direct route to her heart.

At the support group, we pretended not to know each other. I thought it would be sexy having a secret in public, like maybe we'd hold hands on the sly while a mousy sophomore struggled to correctly identify her feelings on the cartoon emotion chart. But facing the truth of how we knew each other was a real boner killer. We both had serious emotional problems we were actively avoiding by distracting ourselves with each other. Eventually we stopped going to group altogether. When given the option between potential sex and talking about my feelings, I chose sex. Between potential sex and class, food, even oxygen, there was no contest. Nevertheless, Nisha was pretty mean, 100 percent unreliable, and never not under the influence of a mélange of uppers and downers, so each day I was met with the challenge of fitting myself into the window of time she was present and lucid. To do this, I kept myself available 24/7, made daily plans with her, and then pretended not to die inside when she inevitably stood me up.

But it was worth it. Changing my Friendster relationship status from "single" to "in a relationship" was the exact moment I felt I'd become a woman. Every fairy tale, Disney film, Jane Austen novel, basically any depiction I'd seen of womanhood, made me believe that you're not complete until you're in a relationship. Being desired seemed to be the most basic requirement for humanity, and I was obsessed with the fact that I'd made it to nineteen without so much as hand holding. What I had with Nisha wasn't ideal, but at least I was somebody's.

One night we were in bed with the lights off when Nisha decided she absolutely had to go out for cigarettes that second. "I won't be able to fall asleep unless I have a cigarette. I'll be right back." But she never came back. Apparently, while she was out "getting cigarettes," she came across a party and got so drunk she urinated in the corner of a stranger's room, at which point she was taken into custody by campus police. I hadn't moved an inch by the time she returned the next morning. After she told me what had happened I tucked her in and cleaned her room.

I tried to introduce her to my parents as "a friend." It must have been so devastatingly clear to them exactly what was going down. They drove up for the day, and she was supposed to join us for dinner, but when we went to her house to pick her up, she wasn't there, didn't even answer the phone. No text, nothing. So I made my parents wait in the car with me for an hour while I tried to track her down. My mom kept gently suggesting we continue on to dinner, and maybe they could meet her next time. "Just five more minutes!" I begged. We waited and waited until she came out. The memory of it still makes my skin crawl.

Eventually, freshman year drew to a close. It was finals week when Nisha woke me up with a phone call in the middle of the night, begging me to come over. I said no. She begged again and again, and I didn't know how to resist—not when being in her bed was so much better than literally any other experience in life. I said I'd come over if she promised to be downstairs at the door. I hated the process of standing there, waiting to be let in; it made me feel pathetic and on display. She agreed, and I walked over in my pajamas. For some reason I still don't fully understand, I brought along the giant, two-foot Pikachu doll I'd taken to sleeping with. Maybe, in my heart of hearts, I knew she wouldn't be downstairs, and a part of me wanted to milk the moment for every last drop of public humiliation.

When she wasn't waiting for me, I called her. I should have turned around, but I couldn't. A morbid part of me wanted to know where the night would take me. I was so new to dating and thought perhaps this kind of shit was par for the course. She said she'd be right down, and I stood there, waiting, continuing to sink down to the most pathetic version of myself, clutching that giant Pikachu. People entered and exited the house. I kept waiting. After about forty-five minutes, the door cracked open and revealed a sliver of her face. "You should go" was all she said before closing it.

I thought that would be the end of it, but then she pulled the ultimate power move. She said she was in love with me. In a voicemail. She delivered it all goofy and affable and self-conscious: "I feel like I'm in *Friends*. Like I'm Ross or something!" She asked me to be her "copilot," and it horrifies me to admit it, but I melted. I immediately called her back and professed my love too because, yeah, this is love, right? You thinking I'm hot, plus big drama?

Sometimes with early gay endeavors, when you're both green and eager and throbbing from the fresh cuts of childhood, it's silently decided that one of you will be the man and the other will be the woman. One of you will lead, and the other will bend and twist to accommodate. One of you will be reckless with the cruelty, and the other will be hungry for it. Maybe this is not a universal experience. Maybe this was just me being nineteen and horny and desperate to please.

The school year ended. I almost failed my classes after phoning in finals. Then I flew to Iran to visit my grandmother while Nisha returned to India. I wrote her emails, detailing the crazy new cast of extended family I'd been introduced to in Tehran. I told her about what it was like to see my language, my face, and my food reflected back to me in the context of the country I belong to but that's never belonged to me. She wrote back and said it was over.

Two weeks into my sophomore year, she called and asked to come over, and I couldn't help myself; I still craved her. I said yes, come over. It was seventy degrees out, but she was wearing a pink beanie I'd once lent her but never had the gall to ask her to return. She mumbled some half-assed apology, we made out, and then we started watching *Kill Bill* in bed. Ten minutes in and she was snoring.

I stared at the hat on her head: it looked like shit. Several of the tiny knit balls that covered it had been torn off, and the pink yarn was a shade or six darker than before. I wanted to curl up and fall asleep next to her, but there was this new voice in my head. It was the tiniest shred of dignity I'd developed in the wake of our breakup. I woke her up and told her to leave. It was the last time we ever spoke. After that, I stopped caring that I hadn't found my place at school. Later that year I found movies, and they were enough as far as companionship goes.

A few years after college, I found photos of Nisha's wedding on Facebook. She was one of the most beautiful brides I'd ever seen. Her hair was shiny and full and back to its natural color; her face looked healthy instead of gaunt as I'd remembered it. She was getting her master's degree and looked genuinely happy.

And standing next to her was her groom, who looked exactly like the real-life embodiment of Beavis from *Beavis and Butt-Head*. I cannot tell you how much joy that brought me.

On the Nose (Job)

"Promise you won't get mad."

For some reason my mom thinks this is a good tactic for presenting an idea that will 100 percent drive you insane.

"I'm not promising that."

"Well, if you're going to get mad, I'm not going to say anything."

This is what makes her approach so clever. You know what she's about to say is going to hit your ears like nails on a chalkboard, but you can't do anything to stop it because now you absolutely *must* find out exactly *how* she's going to offend you, what genre of offense it will be, and how sharp it'll sting.

"You could use a confidence boost, and even though I don't think you necessarily *need* it, I think it could help your mentality, so why don't we just look into getting your nose done?"

I returned home from my freshman year at college a self-pity zombie living from one nap to the next, measuring time through episodes of *The Anna Nicole Smith Show*, and marinating in the kind of heartbreak only a teenager could ferment out of a one-month relationship. Cat Power was the soundtrack to my grief. Have you ever listened to "I Don't Blame You" on loop for eight weeks straight? I dare you to and not give in to the urge to fill your pockets with stones and walk into a river Virginia Woolf–style.

I was taking it pretty fucking hard. The only proof I had that the relationship had even happened was one out-of-focus picture I'd taken of Nisha while she was sleeping. I printed it off my computer so her face took up the entire A4 sheet of paper. I'd stare at it and scan my memories of "us," trying to piece together where I'd gone wrong. The knowledge of the better life I'd so briefly held was excruciating. I'd felt her eyes on me, her hands on my skin, the manic euphoria of waiting outside her door, not knowing what the night would bring but certain that whatever happened, I would be *living*.

This was not living. My parents tiptoed around me. I knew they knew about Nisha. I knew they knew I knew they knew about Nisha. But it was silently understood that the official stance would be feigned ignorance:

"What's wrong?"

"Nothing. I'm just tired."

"We should have your thyroid checked."

"Okay."

We lived in the suburbs, about thirty minutes outside Manhattan, and we didn't know a single person within a twenty-mile radius. My high school, their jobs, and my friends were all in the city, so the house felt like solitary confinement. At night, I'd borrow my dad's ancient Honda Civic and speed across the George Washington Bridge to get to the Lower East Side, where I'd nurse a beer while watching my friend Morgan watch Alice, an older bartender she was infatuated with. The two of them were indulging in one of those infuriating "I like you, you like me, maybe we should? Wait, no, we

definitely shouldn't!" pas de deux, that felt painfully aspirational to me at that time.

I played the chauffeur. You need a ride to Williamsburg
even though it's 2 A.M. and forty minutes out of my way?
Might I volunteer my services? I swear I love fighting to stay
awake while the two of you pretend you're not communicating
through the outer edges of your pinky fingers. I'd drive Alice
to Williamsburg, then drop off Morgan at her parents' place
on the Upper West Side, blasting Mirah all the way.

If we slept together would it make it any better? Mirah sang, as
Morgan ached seeing so much of herself and Alice in the song,
and I for seeing so little of myself in it. If you could burn alive
from jealousy I would have set the Honda Civic and all of the
West Side Highway on fire. I had had a month of being the girl
in the song, and now I was back to this sassy ethnic sidekick
bullshit.

I don't remember how old I was the first time my parents
suggested I get a nose job, but it always felt like the opportunity was sitting on the table, waiting for me to pick it up. Iran
is the nose job capital of the world. My mother, father, aunts,
and grandparents have all gotten nose jobs. In fact, it seems
like a bigger deal to be an Iranian who hasn't had one. It's
barely considered plastic surgery, on par with wearing braces
or highlighting your hair, only it's forever and has a twelve-
month healing period.

At first I'd thought I would break the cycle. At sixteen, I
wrote an article for *The Harriet,* my school's feminist zine
started by a group of intimidating riot grrrl types who wore
padlocks as necklaces. In it, I went "undercover" to blow the
lid off plastic surgery and expose the practice for the evil
crock of shit it was! Which means I went for a consultation in
a place I found in the back of a fashion magazine, then wrote
an article that consisted of one run-on sentence where I

vowed I'd never get a nose job. Actual quote: "I'd no longer be Desiree, but Schmeziree—a weird fake version of myself." The article was strangely prophetic, as the desire to no longer be myself was precisely why I finally decided to get my nose done. Whoever "Schmeziree" was, she had to beat the alternative.

That post-Nisha summer, I was receptive. My guard was down, and I was desperate to feel anything other than heartbreak. For the first time I thought, *Why not have plastic surgery? My face can't get any worse.* But it also seemed a bit pointless, like Febreze-ing a landfill. The discrepancy between me and beauty felt so great I didn't really believe a nose job would do the trick. Still, it was the tiniest bit of action I could take: one step toward a better life.

Knowing when to take my parents' word as fact and when to push back is one of the things that has made being their child a complete mindfuck. Often, they're right. When I was sixteen, my mom got up at five in the morning to take me to Central Park so we could wait in line for tickets to Shakespeare in the Park. *The Seagull* was playing. The way some kids get about comic books, or my mom gets with Baccarat vases, I was obsessed with seeing all of the plays on and off Broadway. Chekhov was my favorite playwright; I loved the way the melodrama and each character's self-pity crescendoed into absurd humor. It felt deeply familiar to me as the daughter of Iranians. Which is why my mom got up at 5 A.M. to wait with me in line in Central Park for the impossible tickets you can't buy and must earn. As the sun rose, word spread through the line that we were too far back to get tickets. Everyone around us packed up and left, but my mom wouldn't budge. I fought her on it. I was mad at the both of us for not getting up earlier, mad at myself for wasting her time, and mad at the lack of autonomy that left me unable to go to the park on my own. For hours I fumed: we're never going to get tickets! And then we did. We were the last in line to get them.*

"Have faith in your mother," she always told me. I have a mother who makes things happen, and she doesn't take no for an answer. She's the kind of person who knows which plastic surgeon is best at which body part, and that's why she chose Dr. Tabriz. Tabriz was known for his noses. She also understood that she'd have to "trick" me into visiting his office. "Let's go so we can laugh at the photos," she'd said when we scheduled the consultation. As we sat in his waiting room, she rolled her eyes at a set of huge fake breasts in the magazine she was flipping through, as if to say, *We're on the same team!*

But when Tabriz used Photoshop to show me how he'd thin out my nose, straighten the bump, and trim the overhanging bit at the bottom, we didn't laugh, we marveled. The change was subtle but undeniable: my eyes looked wider, my face a bit prettier. At the end of the appointment, I watched my mom and the receptionist schedule my surgery, "just to give you the option. He gets booked up so far in advance. We'll cancel it in a week, once you've had time to think about it."

But we didn't cancel it in a week. We snuggled on the couch making fun of the patients on *Dr. 90210* and made no mention of my own Dr. at 10065, until one stiflingly humid August morning I found myself at the Manhattan Eye, Ear & Throat Hospital with my thighs sticking to the plastic waiting room chair. I sat sandwiched between my parents, wondering what had gone through their minds before their respective nose jobs. It felt like an event—it felt *fun.* Nobody was fighting. We were all united on the same team for the first time in I couldn't remember how long.

But the tenor changed once I was separated from them and

* And later that night I slept through 80 percent of the play.

taken past the "no guests allowed" door. I changed into a gown and was hooked up to the anesthesia, but it wasn't until Dr. Tabriz entered the room that the reality of what was about to happen hit me and I dove straight into a heart-pounding, tear-leaking, I-can't-breathe kind of panic. I thought, *I'm going to get a ridiculous, plastic Barbie nose, and it'll sit in the center of my face like a scarlet letter for the rest of my life, announcing: This Girl Was Weak. This girl let her vanity turn her into a walking joke. Why did I let my parents talk me into this? The nose jobs worked for them because they were already attractive, but I'm "the Beast." After this I'll be "the Beast" with a tiny fake nose!* But it was too late. I'd made my choice by not making one. He told me to trust him, but what did this man know about girls like me? Through my tears I begged, "PLEASE DON'T MAKE IT SMALL! I'M TOO BIG FOR A SMALL NOSE!"

They wheeled me into the operating room, where the walls were covered with huge horrifying photos of my face. Before your surgery, you have to go to a professional photographer to take headshots from various angles so the surgeon can remember what your face looked like before he sliced it open and started chiseling away. The last things I remember are the photos and the begging before the anesthesia kicked in and I passed out.

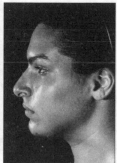

(The aforementioned glamour shots)

In the recovery room, I woke up calm and grateful and high as a motherfucking kite. What is it about drugs that whittles all the resentments away until there's just love? The first thing I heard was my mom's voice: "I saw it before they put the bandages on and it's perfect!"

Dad pulled the car around to the front entrance of the hospital for me like I was a goddamn princess. We stopped at a Korean grocer on the way home and I picked up all the snacks I could get my greedy little hands on. It was still light out when I crawled into my parents' massive marshmallow of a bed with its impossibly soft fresh sheets. It was like being wrapped in a cloud. Their walls were covered in floor-to-ceiling mirrors, so it was more like being in a cloud inside a jewelry box. The mirrors made it feel like you were watching the movie of your life unfold in real time. That day, I stared at my reflection and thought, *This is me on the day of my nose job, swallowed up in bed, blood thick and crusted up each nostril: happy.*

A week later, the cast came off, and two weeks after that I began my sophomore year of college. Nobody noticed I looked any different. I still felt very lonely and very ugly. When I told the Noteables about it, I had to show my profile for them to believe me. Yet there it was: a slope. No more bump.

These days, when someone finds out I've had a nose job, they always ask the same two questions: Do you regret it, and Would you do it again? No, I don't regret it, and no, I wouldn't do it again. I don't think my nose job actually had that much to do with my nose. I was reeling from my first broken heart and my parents wanted to support me, but since my heart had been broken by a girl, we had to pretend it wasn't happening. So they chose to give me a makeover. I went along with it, and for a few weeks in August the three of us were united for what would turn out to be one of the last times in our lives. In the years to come, I would come out of the closet, and they would file for divorce, but that summer we all pretended that mother and father knew best and that a nose job would do the trick of solving my "confidence problem." I'm not mad that it happened. I'm grateful they gave me all of their effort and all of their love.

Recently, I asked my dad what his memory of this time was, and he said, "You wanted to listen to us, but you didn't know the right thing to do." I would say that pretty much sums up our relationship from the time I was fifteen to twenty-five, when I was walking the tightrope between their values and my own instincts. I knew they couldn't yet understand who I was or the world they'd raised me in, but that didn't change the fact that I wanted them to take care of me.

I've lived with this nose for half my life now. Like a tattoo, it reflects a moment in my life that's come and gone. One summer I was nineteen and heartbroken and I put my trust in the people who made me. They did for me what they would have wanted for themselves at a time when I was too scared to make my own choices.

What I Wish
I'd Known at Twenty

- Falling in love is easy. Staying in love is not.
- Your quality of life will improve greatly once you give up on heels and thongs and padded bras and all the shit that makes you feel like you're in drag.
- No matter how much time and money you spend on serums and cleansers and silk pillowcases and prescription creams and antibiotics and Accutane, you will have bad skin. It's not your fault and it's not your pillowcase; it's hormones and it'll pass someday, but not any day soon.
- Everyone thinks everyone else is having better sex than they are.
- You're going to get off the waitlist of an Ivy League graduate school, but you'll be out of the country when they call, and their admissions department will leave you exactly one voicemail, no email, and one week to respond. When you lose your spot, it'll feel like your life is over, but it will be no great loss. I repeat, NO GREAT LOSS.
- Write it all down. Everything.

Cecilia

Part 1: My Blog

The following are actual excerpts from the actual blog I kept during my junior year abroad in London at the URL www.mamalike.blogspot.com.

Wednesday, September 28, 2005

Today was my first day of classes and there was this guy in my French New Wave Cinema class that I got an INSTANT crush on. He has gauged ears and a Mohawk, but not really a Mohawk in the classic sense of a shaved-on-sides/spikes-in-the-middle, but more of a constructed-with-gel, Mohawk-adjacent look.

He's "in" with all the cool film bros, and they all went out for a pint after class. I have this fantasy where me and the Mohawk guy are the "it couple" of the film department. I write scripts that he directs, and I spend most of class on his lap, making out, and everyone's cool with it cause we're so hot and talented and in love. That's the scene that plays in my head, but the scene that plays in real life is my dream dude's off at the pub with all the cool kids while I'm stuck in the post-class film screening, sandwiched between a super dorky Greek guy with bleached tips wearing a tiny Paul Frank backpack that never comes off, and the only other girl in our class, this hella boring Italian who's so shy it seems like she'd burst into flames if you so much as made direct eye contact. Sigh.

Tuesday, October 18, 2005

Today after class, Paul Frank backpack guy invited me to have lunch with him and the film bros! I tried to play it cool like, "Depends. Where are you going?" and then before he could answer I was all, "YES, YES, A THOUSAND TIMES YES!"

The gang consists of five dudes, and all of them think I'm a full-on lesbian because I did that thing I do when I'm trying to be "one of the guys" where I lean into the butch and throw the word "pussy" around gratuitously. All I wanted to do was talk to Mohawkers, but he just wanted to sniff around Cecilia, the Italian girl who looks exactly like a Precious Moments doll and has the personality of a cardboard box.

Tuesday, October 25, 2005

Awesome: Mohawkers helped me pick out movies to rent at the library!

Terrible: Our conversation went:

MOHAWKERS: Is that *Shadow of a Doubt* in your hand? You know, Cecilia LOVES that film? It's her favorite Hitchcock...Have you seen *Le Mépris*? It's so funny, Cecilia hates Godard. She hates Godard, but she LOVES Truffaut! Isn't that WACKY?!

ME: So wacky.

MOHAWKERS: Isn't she the most beautiful, charismatic woman you've ever met?

ME: Sure.

MOHAWKERS: Yeah, but you can't have her! I can't either. She's taken. But they only JUST got together. I doubt it'll last long. It can't last long…right?

Turns out this dude is IN LOVE with the boring Italian girl. We're hanging out one-on-one now, so that's cool, and he keeps alluding to an ambiguously dark past in Thailand, so I'm dying to know what that's all about, but all he wants to do is talk about Cecilia.

Thursday, November 17, 2005

!!!

We kissed, but it wasn't right.

A big group of us are at the pub and Mohawkers keeps getting drunker and drunker and all, "I love you, NY!" (that's what he calls me). "You are so NEW YORK, and at first I thought you'd be stuck up, but you're not and we're so alike!" and I'm thinking, *We can't be that much alike because if we were you'd be kissing me right now.* But he doesn't want to KISS me; he wants to APPRECIATE me. Gross.

We drink absinthe, which tastes like a thousand tiny gnomes hacking away at your esophagus with teeny tiny axes as it trickles down your throat.

"Desiree, that means desire, right? Do you live up to that name?"

"You tell me."

But he doesn't. Instead, he drags us all to his flat in Bethnal Green, and it's not until we're almost there that I realize he's sloppy drunk and it is not hot. He's the kind of drunk where you can see straight through to the worst of a person. He drops his cigarette into his beer while sneaking it onto the bus, then drinks the whole pint down to the end, and while this does nothing to free me of my attraction to him, it does make me start hating us both for it.

When we land at his place, he's all about drinking and playing games that trick you into MORE drinking, and why can't people play more games that trick you into KISSING, which is so much harder to make happen than drinking, but oh wow, the more he drinks the more he touches me! He sits next to me and starts calling me "Desire" instead of "New York," and when we find ourselves alone in the kitchen getting a refill it feels like a moment, so I grab it. I take hold of his collar and kiss him.

Our lips touch for a moment before he pulls back. We both freeze. I think he's going to walk away.

Then, BAM, he GRABS me and throws his face into mine, forceful with the TONGUE and the HANDS GRABBING AT MY ASS. I try to match his pace and mold it into an exchange, but we're on different tracks and he's FULL SPEED AHEAD and then all of a sudden it's over. Sixty seconds into our make-out session he pulls his lips away and yanks us both back into the living room like nothing happened.

Of course Cecilia's sitting there, clear-headed and bright eyed, nursing her second beer as she and Paul Frank Backpack discuss the use of the antihero in Italian cinema as a vehicle to deflect the country's fascist past. Meanwhile, my eyeliner's two inches below my eyelids and my lipstick's all smeared from the idiotic sixty seconds of unsatisfying spit swapping and I can smell my own BO leaking from my T-shirt.

MEANWHILE, Cecilia looks downright angelic, talking with her hands while radiating the glow of a Nivea model. She speaks three languages. She started reading Tolstoy for pleasure at thirteen. She has a boyfriend who's graduated from college and lives in Bristol and is probably better than all of us because she'd never throw herself at a shitfaced animal who'd just swallowed a cigarette.

I'm starting to think the world is divided into the Cecilias and the Desirees: the pretty, normal, sweet, quiet, nonabrasive girls who act as a blank canvas for men to project their fantasies onto, and the girls who are too much. I sat in the living room and said nothing for the rest of the night as I watched her perfect face and her perfect hair and her infrequent but perfect words melt the hearts of all the boys around us.

Then, I took the 25 night bus four stops in the wrong direction before I realized I was heading to Oxford Circus.

Tuesday, November 22, 2005

The film bros came to my place last night and I kinda HAD to invite Cecilia because she was there when the plans were being made. Then she insisted on coming downstairs with me to get food because of course she's better at hosting even when I'm the host. And the next thing I know we're having this big talk about life how we both kinda wish we were the other person.

WHAAAAAAAA??????

It turns out, this whole time that I've been eaten alive with jealousy for this girl, SHE'S been jealous of ME! Isn't that insane?!

Apparently she sees me as outspoken and opinionated, and for some reason she sees these as good qualities?? (I don't get it either.)

She was too scared to speak to me because she has no confidence, which is so strange because I have no confidence, but it makes me speak WAY TOO MUCH! I can't tell if it's deeply comforting or deeply depressing that even the "perfect" girls hate themselves and wish they were someone else. Whichever it is, I'm SO HAPPY we finally spoke!!! She's actually pretty cool and funny! I had no idea because she was too insecure to speak!

Part 2: My Friend

The first time I laid eyes on Cecilia was on the first day of my junior year abroad in London. We were both twenty years old. She was standing outside French New Wave Cinema, with big doe-eyes, sideswept bangs, and the thickest lashes I've yet to see on a human without the aid of an aesthetician. I took one look at her and thought, "Fuck that bitch."

It was 2005. I weighed about fifty pounds more than my doctor wanted me to, had sweat stains on all my shirts, and wore a tutu like it was a skirt in an attempt at hipster chic that made me look less like Carrie Bradshaw and more like that hippo in *Fantasia*. All I wanted was to lose my "man virginity," but seducing a man was proving to be a challenge, as my go-to move was to emasculate dudes with what I thought was pithy Hepburn/Bogart banter but what I'm pretty sure actually came off as unpleasantness from a women's college–educated lesbian who wouldn't shut the fuck up. Cecilia's social strategy was to only speak when spoken to, and it was far more successful.

In class, she'd reference European directors with an encyclopedic knowledge I'd reserved for shows from ABC's 1996 TGIF lineup. She drew ties between the films we watched and the political climate of the time and place they'd been made. There was never a moment she wasn't soft-spoken, pretty, humble, and sweet. She was the embodiment of every feminine trope I failed to emulate, and I hated her for it.

Every girl I met felt like competition. They were all obstacles between me and whichever guy was standing within a two-mile radius. I had started feeling this way around thirteen, when men's eyes first began to linger. It became a game: Who can get the most eyes on them? Of course it was a game I never won but tried to play nonetheless. When I met Cecilia, I was in a new country and desperate to reinvent myself as the kind of girl I'd worshipped in high school, the one for whom every man was a potential target. Or was it vice versa? Either way, I found it something to aspire to.

When it came to my dealings with other women, hatred and admiration lived in such close proximity that it was hard to tell them apart. I still have to make the conscious choice to be a fan of the other person instead of allowing her gifts to become a direct reflection of my personal failings. On the night we had our first real conversation, Cecilia disarmed me. She waved a white flag by making it clear that she admired me, and I decided that if I couldn't be like her, at least I could enjoy being liked by her.

What I hadn't known until we started talking was that she'd grown up chubby with an unfortunate overbite and was only just beginning to find herself the subject of male attention. What made her my hero was that she couldn't have cared less about it. In fact, once I had her friendship, Mohawkers and the pursuit of the male gaze began to feel like a waste of time.

Her name is spelled "Cecilia," but it's pronounced Chichilia because she refused to acquiesce to the English way of saying it, and she's right, the Italian CH in place of C is far superior. She talks way too fast, like one word is shoving the next out of her mouth and they're running from a fire. She hangs her clothes up like she's mad at them: collars flipped under, sleeves inverted, all facing different directions and all on wire hangers.* She cries easily, but never longer than thirty seconds, she's always multitasking, and when she finds herself at a party she gravitates toward the person with the least status in the room.

She's an intrinsically lovable person; you feel the warmth and innate selflessness radiating off her from the moment you say hello. What's weird about Cecilia is that, yes, she's one of those rare, sacred, *good* people, and yet it's the least notable thing about her. She's also an intellectual with impeccable taste and a sharply dark sense of humor. I've never known a person to have the sweetness *and* the talent. Her Italian accent will seduce you, her sincerity will endear her to you, and then her intelligence will carry the conversation straight to the core of what matters. Once I began benefiting from those qualities instead of competing with them, my life transformed.

Because I liked her so much, and she seemed to like me just as much, being friends gave me permission to like myself. We were so different: she was a painfully shy introvert raised in Milan by intellectuals who put Tolstoy in her hands, while I was a loudmouthed extrovert desperate for attention, raised in New York by conservative Iranians who parked me in front of the television and led me to believe you could get pregnant from kissing. Yet somehow we saw the world through the same lens. I think it's because we both knew what it felt like to be invisible, even if we reacted to it in opposite ways: it made me crave attention and power, while it gave Cecilia the ability to see through them. She's able to spot greatness in the least shiny people. The best gift of my life was when she saw it in me.

---

* To be fair, I don't think *Mommie Dearest* was big in Italy.

We became instant best friends. Together, we had the most fun I'd ever had, even though we never really "did" anything. She'd host me daily in her studio apartment, and I'd make us the same shitty stir-fry noodles that never ceased to amaze her, night after night. We watched movies, alternating between high and low—*Never Been Kissed* and Kiarostami. We each worked on developing a "signature style," Cecilia with these tiny feathered clip-on hats from Spitalfields Market, and me with vintage scarves I'd tie around my neck in a nod to Faye Dunaway in *Bonnie and Clyde* that made me look more like a baby wearing a bib. Eventually, we discovered the Photo Booth function on her Mac, which consumed whatever time was left over between school, movies, and noodles. And that's how we settled into our twenties: communicating mostly in movie quotes, laughing noodles out our noses. Two complete beginners, each the other's greatest fan.

I'd had friends before her, but friends with caveats. For some reason they were always blonde, and I'd trick them into intimacy with borderline-sociopath techniques like mirroring opinions and replacing my personality with relentless niceness. Sarah Feldman wore pink PUMAs with pink skirts and glitter on her eyes, so *I* wore pink PUMAs with pink skirts and glitter on my eyes. She smoked cigarettes and shoplifted from the Urban Outfitters on Seventy-second Street, so I did too. It was all very *Talented Mr. Ripley* in both my doglike obedience and suffocated rage. Meeting Cecilia marked the first time I'd stepped into a friendship on equal footing. We each wished we could be more like the other but accepted that it wasn't in either of our natures, so we settled on coexisting.

Being together made me want to write. More specifically, it made me want to write to make her laugh. When I got to London, I'd started taking notes on whatever struck me: my dormmate's habit of narrating his inner monologue out loud as he stomped through the hallway and planned his walking tours, British people's way of calling you "mate" when they really mean "Go fuck yourself," the tableau I came across one early Sunday morning of pigeons flocking to fresh vomit outside King's Cross as barefoot girls in sparkling dresses stumbled to their trains home. I felt like I could pull together my observations to write something she might like. So, parked on her Ikea foldout couch, I assembled the notes I'd been taking into a script about three couples at a bar and based all of them on romantic mishaps I'd gotten myself into, including my love triangle with Mohawkers and Cecilia. I called it *Two Drink Minimum* and forced our classmates (including Mohawkers) to shoot it as our production class project (and my first short film).

In the years that followed, I moved back to the States and she stayed in London, but every six months one of us would fly to see the other, and it would feel as if no time had passed. She eventually went from being my best friend to my producer and then my writing partner.

One of my all-time favorite films is *Muriel's Wedding*, an Australian comedy where a complete loser (Muriel) reinvents herself after making her first real friend (Rhonda). There's a scene early in the film, when they've just met and they're lying on the beach late one night staring up at the stars as they share a bottle of Moët and Muriel asks, "Do you ever think you're nothing? Sometimes I think I'm nothing." To which Rhonda replies, "You're not nothing Muriel, you're amazing!"

The camera's tight on Muriel's face as she takes this in, and you get the sense that, for the first time in her life, she can see her own potential through another person's eyes. That's exactly what it was like meeting Cecilia in 2005 when we were both twenty-year-old virgins* with no sense of who we were or what we wanted. She introduced me to myself. I'd been so conditioned to think I needed a man to jump-start my life, when all I needed was someone who spoke my language.

Sometimes I still can't believe my luck. I wish I could go to my teenage self and tell her, "Somewhere in Italy there's a dyslexic cinephile with a terrible bowl cut who sees the world the way you do. You will meet and make each other laugh, and she'll help you redefine your definition of cool to include yourself. And you won't be alone anymore."

---

* Yes, I'd been with Nisha, but I decided I was a virgin until I had sex with a man (and of course the moment I had sex with a man I realized I definitely had not been a virgin).

A Tragic Bunch of
Basic Bitches

It's difficult to find a photo of me as a child without something soft, delicious, and gooey clenched in one fist. I had a halo of curls and thick rolls of flesh gathered around my middle. I've been told that offering me food was the only way to get me to come to you, so in many of the photos I'm perched on someone's lap with cream all over my face. One of my earliest memories is making a huge fuss over having had only two meals one day and refusing to go to sleep until my mom promised I'd get a fourth meal the next day to compensate.

I can't pinpoint the exact moment I began to feel that something was drastically wrong with my body and that the remedy was to start messing with my food intake, but the two feel intrinsically linked. I remember standing in a JCPenney dressing room at twelve, trying on dresses to wear to my first dance, when one of the adults in my life stared at my reflection, pinched my stomach, and said, "You'd be perfect if you just lost this."

Shit.

It never left me. Every single mirror. Every single photo. Every single bite. You'd be perfect if you just

lost

this.

Ten years later I was about to start film school, but I wasn't quite the butterfly I'd hoped I'd have transformed into post teenage cocoon. I knew I was a late bloomer, but I kept thinking, *Shouldn't I have bloomed by now?* Everyone I knew had come into their own at college. My friend Morgan cut her hair off and became captain of the rugby team at Oberlin. My friend Halley starred in avant-garde theater productions at Wesleyan with visionaries who practiced fire-breathing for fun. I left college without a single friend or accolade. I saw grad school as a fresh canvas, but I worried that if I went on the way I was, I'd be destined for another four years of mediocrity and anonymity. So I decided I needed to lose fifty pounds.

I figured if I got thin it would make me beautiful, and that walking into film school beautiful would elevate me to the highest level of the school's social ladder, and that the highest level of the social ladder would be where all the best filmmakers would fraternize. So, in the months leading up to my first day of school, I limited eating to the moments I'd "earned" it, when I was lightheaded and my insides felt like they were folding in on themselves. I created rules about how much of the meal should remain on the plate when the fork went down. I championed the "good" foods, shunned the "bad," and invested in a wide array of laxatives.

But I had no discipline, I never had, not with the cello and not with anorexia. By starving myself, I only managed to further fetishize food. By the end of the week I'd be hit with a deep manic throbbing of want for all the things, all at once. I was ravenous, but it wasn't just my stomach that was empty; my heart, my ego, and my mommy issues all needed feeding, and there was no floor to the depth of that hunger, so I shoveled the food in until I forgot how to stop. The food danced from my hand to my mouth to my throat without my even tasting it: hand, mouth, throat. Hand. Mouth. Throat. I kept eating and eating until I'd fall into a trance where it felt like my body was acting independently of my brain—like my brain had looked around and said, *Yikes, I'm outta here* and started watching from the ceiling. I kept chewing and chewing until I thought I was going to burst right down the middle like that scene in *Alien*.

I hate food. I hate how it's not a choice, that you crave it morning, noon, and night, every single day of your entire stupid life. I hate the gap of time between when you're eating and when you're satiated, so you're never quite sure when to put the fork down. I hate that there are so many options of what to eat and that some are good and some are bad and it's never totally clear which is which.

I love food. It's my favorite reward, my favorite consolation prize, my favorite way to express love or relish boredom. It's the best pacifier to whatever feeling you're drowning in. I love the moment something warm and perfectly seasoned enters your mouth for the first time, and you know there's a whole plate of it waiting for you. I love the crunch of a perfectly cooked *tahdig* between your teeth. I love the slimy texture of the aubergine in a stew: how it falls apart on your tongue and feels gooey, like an overripe banana, but tastes creamy like bone marrow.

But more than I love the pleasure of eating, I hate the fullness and the guilt it shepherds in. The fullness is the worst sensation I know. When I was twenty-two and weeks away from starting grad school, it felt like if I didn't get rid of the fullness, the shame would swallow me whole. I'd crammed it in, and now I had to yank it out.

Vomiting's exhausting. It's feral and violent and makes every inch of you rev up until you're leaking tears and sweat while shivering with cold. You keep going until your whole body goes limp, arms wrapped in an embrace with the porcelain. This is what you deserve after what you did. Every time it happened, I'd think, *Oh shit, I didn't see that coming*, until it was *Oh shit, I didn't see that coming* several times a day.

It felt like the food was killing me, each bite making me actively more disgusting: the gluten, the pesticides, the legumes, the nightshades all rendering me fat, stupid, weak. Eating meat is bad for you *and* the environment. Actually, no, scratch that, you should be eating *just* meat and nothing else. And only eat it from eleven to seven so your body runs out of calories and starts burning fat. But also you should be eating breakfast as soon as you wake up so your metabolism doesn't slow down, and when you *do* eat just go ahead and juice everything and drink that instead of food. Hold up! It turns out all the nutrition is in the pulp—JUST GIVE ME THE RULES AND I WILL FOLLOW THEM.

A few months into my first year at NYU, I found myself sitting across from a psychologist at the NYU Health Center. I was there because when you go to the Health Center for anything—from birth control to a flu shot—you have to fill out a form where you rate how you're feeling, and (surprise) I have no poker face, even in print. I give it all away, too much, too quick, and that routine half-page survey ratted me out.

"Do you ever purge after meals?"

"Yeah, but only sometimes. It's not like I have an eating disorder."

Jesus, psychologists can be such drama queens.

She gave me an article about the Minnesota Starvation Experiment. In 1944, the University of Minnesota conducted a study to analyze the mental and physical effects of food deprivation in an attempt to figure out the best way to help famine victims after the war. They took a group of conscientious objectors and observed them eating normally for three months, then severely restricted their food intake for six months, to the point where each participant lost 25 percent of his body weight. After that, they transitioned to three months of restricted rehabilitation, where food was slightly increased. Then they ended the experiment with eight weeks of unrestricted eating. The results were clear across the board: all participants went completely batshit.

They binged (sometimes over eleven thousand calories in a day), they purged, they fantasized about food and drooled over cookbooks as though they were porn. When they couldn't get their hands on any actual food, they stole and hoarded food-related objects like cups and coffeepots and hot plates. Once they were allowed to eat again, they never felt full because when you mess with someone's food intake, it ruins their ability to feel satiated. By the end of the experiment, all of them put on more weight than they had going in, most of them complained of feeling fat when they were underweight, three of them left their careers to become chefs, and one guy began carrying candy bars in his pockets at all times.

I read the article and realized, *Holy shit, I've handicapped myself.* I'd always considered myself more of a failed dieter than someone with an actual eating disorder. I'd thought that I lacked discipline and that if I could just build the strength of character to commit to eating the bare minimum, I'd be okay. The study made me realize I was being delusional. It was empirical proof that restrictive eating atrophies your brain and your body. It carried an extra air of legitimacy for me because the subjects were male, and I found myself unable to blame their failure on lack of willpower. So it turned out I was bulimic *and* sexist.

I tried to stop. For two years I went to group therapy, nutritionists, and even Overeaters Anonymous, but nothing worked for me. Sometimes, when I couldn't find a nearby Overeaters Anonymous meeting, I'd go to AA instead. I was always jealous of the alcoholics. Being addicted to food felt about as dangerous as being addicted to stamp collecting or being addicted to picking your nose and eating it. It felt like the alcoholics had the better stories, the hotter people, and the very tangible rule of NO DRINKING. I don't mean to belittle it: the feat of not drinking can be Herculean, but I envied the infrastructure they had in place for achieving it. A clear plan of attack: no drugs, no booze, follow these rules, call this sponsor, go to that meeting. In any city, in any country, you're going to find a room and a community that gets it, because if they're a friend of Bill's, they're a friend of yours.

Food addiction, on the other hand, has no clear boundaries. You have to consume your drug on a daily basis and renegotiate the terms of your separation. I'd binge and then I'd *have* to purge, and then the shame of it would make me binge again. Then purge again. It became routine and consistent, yet somehow shocking every time, like waves at the beach that sneak up from behind and smack you off your feet, then suck you in. Every single day. Eventually I stopped being able to tell if I was hungry or full. Then I stopped being able to keep food down, no matter what amount I'd eaten. I'd messed with my gag reflex so much it went into permanent ON mode.

When I think of the worst of my bulimia, I think of Jamie Oliver. *Jamie Oliver's Food Revolution* was a reality show where British chef and TV personality Jamie Oliver visited American schools to prove the children didn't have a fighting chance at overcoming their doughy inadequacy because their school lunches consisted of fatty poison laced in high-fructose corn syrup. So Jamie decided to devote himself to saving the

children through their lunch ladies and starting a "food revolution."

I would watch this show for hours while gorging myself on
anything I could get my hands on without having to leave the
house. I'd go back and forth from my room to the kitchen,
grabbing food to shove down my throat in a brain-dead, hyp-
notic daze, taking breaks only to puke into cups I hid under the
bed until my roommates were gone, at which point I'd take
trips back and forth to the bathroom to empty them while
brainstorming excuses in case someone came home and caught
me carrying a cup of my own vomit.

I saw myself in those obese children and the rolls of flesh
hanging over the tops of their cargo shorts. Every insult
hurled at those small-town fatties ricocheted right off the TV
and landed on me. I knew that in my heart of hearts I would
rather die thin than live fat.

At some point around episode 6, two years into the constant bingeing and purging and group therapy and nutritionists and Overeaters Anonymous, I reached my limit. I couldn't
keep living like my body was holding me hostage and every
menu was a catch-22. I couldn't even watch an NBC reality
show without taking the child obesity epidemic personally. I
decided that more than being thin or popular or even a successful filmmaker, I really just wanted to stop doing this to
myself. So I started the intake process at a rehabilitation center
called Renfrew.

The first step of "getting better" was having to perform my
life story six different times to six different doctors over the
course of six ninety-minute appointments: from the NYU
Health Center psychologist who referred me to Renfrew, to the
general practitioner who performed the pre-intake physical, to
the intake evaluation therapist, to the nutritionist, to the psy-

chiatrist, to the psychologist they assigned me for the duration
of treatment.

With each meeting, you start to feel where your audience
engages and where they detach—when the traumatic childhood breadcrumbs align with the clues they're digging for, and
when you're wasting time getting lost in your own self-pity. By
the end of my six-appointment run, I'd pulled together a pretty
tight one-woman show of THE WORST THINGS THAT
EVER HAPPENED TO ME, from being voted the Ugliest
Girl at Horace Mann to the cups of vomit to all the really ugly
shit that I have *just* enough propriety to keep out of this book. I
laid it all at their feet and begged them to lock me away in a
residential facility, but they were all, "Dude, don't flatter yourself," and I was referred to Renfrew's outpatient program,
which met three days a week in midtown Manhattan.

The vibe at IOP (Intensive Outpatient) was children's day-
care meets prison: a wicker basket full of cozy beige blankets,
plus the occasional supervised bathroom visit. You'd give up
your free will when you walked through the door, only to get
it right back again upon leaving, and there was something incredibly disorienting about that. We were all women, though
our ages varied, and most of the patients had just been released
from an inpatient facility in Philadelphia.

At first, I was awed by their hairy arms, bony knees, and
pronounced clavicles. It felt like they'd succeeded where I'd
failed. Maybe that's what made this so on-brand for me: I'm
bisexual, not gay. Iranian American, not Iranian. Bulimic, not
anorexic. Always one step away from the real McCoy. At least
I'm consistent. Anorexics are perfectionists. Bulimics are perfectionists with bad execution. We'd been competing to be the
thinnest and the hungriest our whole lives, and now we were
in competition to win at recovery.

Everyone at IOP felt like a character from a different genre. There was Kaia, a teeny-tiny, wise-beyond-her-years thirteen-year-old with a buzz cut and a thick coat of fur on her arms that made her look like a tiny monkey. She never spoke, she just stared back at you with dead hollow eyes, and a good 60 percent of my mental energy was spent speculating wildly over what razor-sharp judgments she was formulating. When she was forced to contribute, her words painted the picture of a calm, insightful little genius who was so frail she could barely hold her head up.

Rebecca was in her midtwenties and wore a uniform of skintight jeans and modest high-neck tops that did nothing to camouflage her crowning jewel: a gloriously massive set of tits. She had a rich old man boyfriend who would whisk her off to Brazil or Nice on a moment's notice. There was a naive generosity about her that seemed incongruent with her looking like Jessica Rabbit's human incarnation. One time she brought me a bottle of the Kérastase hair oil she used religiously because I'd complimented her hair's sheen. If we'd met in the real world, my jealousy would have squashed my ability to see her humanity. But in the bizarre alternate universe occupying the midtown airspace between Park and Madison, I had the privilege of watching her lose her shit over an extra hummus portion, silently sob through dinner, then stay behind at the table for the mandatory standoff that followed all unfinished Renfrew meals: girl versus paper cup of vanilla Ensure. That shit will humanize anyone.

Alex was from South America—I never found out exactly where. Every day she wordlessly sank into the couch, hugged a throw pillow tight to her middle, and stared out at the rest of us with the puffy, red, swollen eyes of a person who'd just cried so hard and so long that she was beyond verbal communication. She had habitual rock-bottom face. She only spoke when pressed, and when she did, I could taste her sadness.

Chloe was the only obese patient during my time at Renfrew. I found myself watching her, trying to understand what it would feel like to be the fattest person in a room of people obsessed with fat. What was it like waking up in her body? Waking up in mine felt like a sick nightmare. From the moment I saw her I knew she looked familiar, but it wasn't until two weeks later that I realized her face was an exact carbon copy of La Saraghina in Fellini's *8½*, wide and expressive, with high sharp eyebrows and a great big mouth that was either upturned into a huge grinning smile or sunken into a deep frown. The way she styled herself was emblematic of her personality: sickly saccharine sweetness wrapped in Shirley Temple ringlets, caked-on rosy cheeks, and floral sweater sets. I suspected she felt she was too fat to be allowed to be anything other than nice. I thought this because that's how I'd navigated most of my adolescence (and won the award for "Nicest Camper" at Pierce Camp Birchmont in 1994).

They couldn't have been more different from one another, and yet they were all the exact same person: the girl trying to take up the least amount of space in the room. The girl who would chop her arm off to avoid the slightest whiff of conflict. They'd sit around the dinner table, cutting their burritos into teeny-tiny pieces between constant sips of water as they made mind-numbingly dull small talk about *The Bachelor* because reality TV was the only subject that wouldn't be construed as triggering by staff. In therapy, they'd break down their lives and their pasts and their goals for the future, and I'd think, *What a tragic bunch of basic bitches.* I wanted to shake each one of them and scream, *Dude. You're making yourself sick and it's not cute. Stop. Your body's fine the way it is. YOU'RE WASTING YOUR LIFE, YOU FUCKING DUMBASS.*

It took me weeks to realize they were all me. I was staring at thirteen Desirees. All the idiotic things they were doing and

saying were the exact same idiotic things I was doing and saying to myself. Everything they needed to hear, *I* needed to
hear. That's one of the magical things about rehab; you think
you're hiding among strangers, but as you unravel the story of
each of their lives, you get closer and closer to understanding
your own.

Even the outliers: Grace was a sixty-five-year-old public
school teacher with a binge-eating problem and only sharp
edges. No friends, no family, no warmth. It felt like she wanted
to transmit her misery out to the world like a venereal disease.
On more than one occasion I watched her have a toddler-style
tantrum over peanut butter. She was mad about the brand
(Skippy), and the paltry serving size (one tablespoon): "This is
RIDICULOUS. I WANT more PEANUT butter!" She kept
letting her crazy show. The rest of us were determined to tuck
it in and hide it away until the perfect storm of stressors sent
us into a full-on breakdown, but not Grace. Grace did not give
a shit. I kept thinking of her students, and whether or not it
was their fault that she was so bitter. I don't think I ever saw
her smile. I'd watch her face twist further into a scowl and
think, *That's me in forty years if I don't drop this shit.*

My parents got a full serving of Grace when they came in
for family night. Each Wednesday, for the final hour of program, we could invite our loved ones to join group therapy.
Grace hated family night. She was angry about its very existence. Her family was cruel, and she was alone in the world.
She was about two acts into her FUCK THIS SHIT soliloquy
when, out of nowhere, my mom grabbed both of Grace's hands
with her own. Tears fell down her cheeks as she said, "I know
they hurt you and made so, so many mistakes, but I know they
loved you. Kids don't come with a manual."

The whole room fell quiet. My mom had spoken with so
much vulnerability and heart. I'd assumed she would cling to

the role of victim and view Renfrew through that lens. Instead, she pled her case as a parent. She was holding Grace's hands, but the apology was for me. She'd tried her best, and it wasn't perfect. And she was sorry.

Grace abruptly snatched her hands away and told Mom to go fuck herself.

We laughed about it later, as my parents drove me back to Brooklyn, over an hour out of their way home. I was so overcome with love for them, so lucky to be theirs. We sped down the West Side Highway, all green lights and no traffic, and my mom held my hand from the front seat the entire drive.

Finally, there was Jocelyn, a seventeen-year-old Long Island princess who was a hybrid of my worst teenage triggers: Horace Mann mean girl aesthetic paired with the power-hungry swagger of the Iranian kids I grew up with. You could tell she was the leader of the second-most-popular clique at school. Her long silky hair was ironed, and she kept flipping it from one side of her face to the other, methodically, like a metronome: left, right, left, right. Like all tristate area popular girls of the time, she wore a uniform of 7 for All Mankind jeans, Petit Bateau tops, and a teeny-tiny Coach bag just big enough to hold one Stila lip gloss and a cellphone.

That fucking cellphone.

She had it with her at all times, even though the rules were NO PHONES. The rest of us had silently agreed that obsessive rule following and wanting to "get better" were the social currency, but Jocelyn didn't seem to be aware of the pact. Her phone was glued to her hand throughout the day. She'd show me a steady stream of topless eighteen-year-old-boy selfies, saying all the guys at her school were after her. She once walked into dinner bragging about how she had "the metabolism of a Jew in a concentration camp" after being so anorexic for so many years.

Jocelyn and I got into it one day when I brought up her cellphone use in group therapy. I felt it was inappropriate; she felt I should mind my own fucking business. I felt that if she was on her phone during group therapy, then it *was* my business. And *she* felt that maybe she should kick my ass. She got up real close and threatening and called me a "stupid bitch." Typically, that would be the moment I'd shrink and backpedal to try to de-escalate the situation, but for the first time in my life I looked a bully in the face and said, "You don't scare me" (under the watchful eye of a psychologist referee). She was seventeen, and I was a grown woman, but it felt like a watershed moment.

Rebecca, Chloe, and a handful of the other girls started crying. Everyone's individual trauma buttons were being pressed, and there was something a bit magnificent about watching the room unravel and having to sit with that discomfort. This is the genius of group therapy: it's at its best when you bring conflict into the room and face your anger in a controlled environment with the aid of a counselor at the wheel. Sarah, an exercise bulimic who couldn't sleep unless she'd done enough cardio to counteract every calorie she'd eaten that day, gave me a look of awe that I'll never forget. She really hated Jocelyn. We all did. But nobody had ever confronted her.

When it was time to stop going to Renfrew, I felt ready. I hadn't purged in the eight weeks of treatment, and I haven't to this day. I left feeling like Dorothy in the last act of *The Wizard of Oz*, when she realizes she could have gone home all along; she just had to click her heels. The power to recover was always within me. There was no secret, no magic diet, no formula to "getting better." I just had to stop hurting myself. That said, learning what exactly constitutes "hurting yourself" is a tricky thing. I needed to watch a room full of women self-sabotage over and over, like it was a horror film where all I could do was scream at the screen, "Don't go into the cellar!"

When I think of Renfrew, I think of Ensure and heavy cotton blankets and plastic Ikea measuring spoons in peanut butter jars. I think about my mom's hand holding mine from the front seat as my dad whizzed down the West Side Highway, and how much love it must have taken to stomach family night on a Wednesday. I think about Kaia's furry arms, Jocelyn's hair flips, Rebecca's massive tits, and Chloe's perfect A-line skirts with the matching sweater sets, and I think about how, for a brief period of time, we were all united in our goal of getting "better," even though none of us really knew what "better" even looked like. Together, we chased the hope that someday we would.

Would Wong Kar Wai
Approve That Frame?

During the years I was in grad school at NYU, I spent the majority of my waking hours at the Tisch School of the Arts building at 721 Broadway. I'd often sit glued to an edit station for twenty-four hours straight, leaving once around 2 A.M. for borscht at Veselka. Then sometime around dawn, I'd inevitably crash the system and lose all my work because I never quite figured out how to set up the automatic backup on Avid. It's not with false modesty that I say I wasn't "one to watch." I was more like one of those reject auditions on *American Idol* that goes viral. You know, the ones you see and think, *There's no way that person's delusional enough to think they have talent.* I was the William Hung of NYU's grad film program. Nevertheless, I had this deep-in-my-bones conviction I was meant to be a filmmaker, even if nobody agreed with me.

There was only one assignment during the second year of school: make a ten-minute film. It sounds simple, but accomplishing this became one of the hardest things I've ever done in my life. The film was meant to be the calling card that would establish your voice, tone, and style and get you into Sundance. At Sundance, you'd secure financing for a full-length feature film based on the short. Once you won Sundance with the feature based on the short, you'd sign a three-picture deal with Focus Features, and the next thing you know, you'd be dating Michelle Williams. This trajectory shall henceforth be referred to as "the Cary Fukunaga."

When I was at NYU, Cary Fukunaga had just achieved this meteoric rise to glory with his second-year film, and it was the only example any of us had of how to go from directing student to actual director. The fact that he'd recently been in the very same program made the dream feel both tauntingly attainable and impossibly out of reach. Even his name felt aspirational and mysterious, like a high-end French perfumery that was somehow also Japanese.

This short film needed to be cool and edgy, while also deep and moving, but ALSO hilarious, and if it wasn't all of those things, I'd have no future. For the story, I decided to expose my darkest secret: my nose job. Not that many people knew that I'd had plastic surgery. It was something I was incredibly ashamed of, so it felt like fertile ground to build a film on. I decided if I was going to make a film about my nose job, I'd have to write my parents into it, because then I could make their characters speak Farsi, and if there was one thing I knew about filmmaking it was that foreign language films could be vague, confusing, and mind-achingly boring and you still had to like them (or else you were trash). And, after months of brainstorming, I decided to call it *Nose Job*, because I am bad at titles.

On the first day of shooting, I couldn't approve a single frame my cinematographer offered up. The clock was ticking, lunch was approaching, and I just kept staring at the monitor, paralyzed, asking myself the same question on loop: *Would Wong Kar Wai approve this frame?* My gut said no. *What about*

Bergman, would he approve? Again, no. I kept making tiny adjustments, moving a light, changing a shirt, changing a lens, hoping to arrive at an image that looked like it came from the mind of an actual director, not some girl who had no idea what she was doing. I inched through the whole shoot like that. I never once asked myself, *What would* you *approve of? What's in* your *head?*

The film was a mess. I made all of the rookie mistakes. Instead of sticking with the fact that I was nineteen and somewhat willing when I went under the knife, I made the lead character fourteen and practically mute. I did that thing where you make the lead (who is clearly based on you) the least interesting part of the script because every first-time filmmaker thinks they're inherently compelling, no questions asked. There's an art to rendering yourself on-screen: you have to boil your personality down to a caricature and then add a healthy dose of whatever your own cocktail of crippling fragility is. It's a skill I've honed over decades and have yet to perfect, but man, with that first film I didn't even come close.

I did that other inexperienced filmmaker thing where you forget to shoot any establishing shots of the locations, so the film lacks any sense of time and place. And in an attempt at "nuance," I kept the script ambiguous and unstructured with no clear story, goal, or resolution, so the film came out with no beginning, middle, or end. Here's a play-by-play: a girl's mom makes her go to the doctor. Doctor tells her to get a nose job. Her parents tell her she should get a nose job. She gets a nose job and cries in the operating room as they're administering the anesthesia. Later, she wakes up in her parents' marshmallow of a bed, surrounded by mirrors, looks at her own reflection, bruised and battered, and smiles.

The worse offense of all was that I let myself get peer-pressured into spending a small fortune of student loan money* on buying and developing Super 16 film because the vibe at school was all, "Real filmmakers shoot celluloid, not digital." That is 100 percent not true. If I'd shot on digital, I would have been able to do more takes and make a better movie. I had no artistic attachment to analog film; I was just scared of not being taken seriously.

Surprise, surprise: *Nose Job* did not have the Fukunaga factor. The film was neither bad nor good, just inconsequential. I spent a thousand dollars on submission fees to over thirty film festivals and was rejected by all but one: a tiny women's film festival in Hollywood (Florida).

I flew out to the Hollywood (Florida) film festival premiere with my mother, who starred in the film as . . . the mother. She had absolutely no desire to be on camera, but I forced her into the role the night before the shoot, when my lead actress backed out and I took the news so hard I decided I had no choice but to drop out of school. Time and time again, my mother put herself through hell in an effort to teach me to never give up.

When we got to Hollywood (Florida), we realized that it wasn't really a film festival as much as some screenings at a high school gym. We never managed to find a single person who worked there, just a few friendly volunteers handing out voting cards who were eager to inform us that the celebrity guest judge that year was the woman who played Mrs. Winslow on *Family Matters.*†

We spent three days wandering Hollywood (Florida), searching for screenings, getting lost, and finding ourselves desperate and starving with nowhere to go but Hooters. *Nose Job* played on our last day in town as part of the student shorts

---

* That I'm still paying off to this day.

† The original, not the one who took over for the last season.

program. I knew it was a student program when I applied, but I hadn't realized it was a *high school* student shorts program until we were seated and saw I was one of three people in that auditorium old enough to vote.

The program lasted over three hours. *Nose Job* played dead last, and as my opening title came on-screen, the entire audience collectively decided it was time to leave. How could I blame them? I'd been ready to bail on the screening two hours earlier. For the entire ten minutes of the film's run time, my mom kept shouting, "IT'S NOT OVER!" at random teenagers stepping over her to exit the cinema. Bless her for her outrage that day. Bless her for asking questions during the Q&A, where fifteen directors addressed an audience of four. *Nose Job* and the Hollywood (Florida) Women's Film Festival were these big flashing neon signs that said: GIVE UP. On my way out of the screening, an usher stopped me: "Make sure you don't leave without talking to *Mother Winslow*. You gotta give her your business card and network that shit!" I remember thinking, *Nope. This is not a dream I should be pursuing anymore.*

On the drive to the airport, I was crying so hard I could barely get the words out: "Why did I delude myself into thinking I could be a filmmaker? What am I going to do with the rest of my life?" My mother allowed me to cry for exactly five minutes before she told me to pull myself together. She reminded me of the night we'd camped out for tickets to Shakespeare in the Park, and how I'd wanted to give up the second someone told us we were too far back in line. She reminded me that we weren't quitters. It simply was not allowed. I could feel sorry for myself for the length of that drive, and then I had to get on with it.

My mother, the hero—the woman who shaped me and never lost faith. How come it's so hard to see your mother's greatness when it's in action, but so easy to spot the deficits the second they reveal themselves? In that moment I understood what it was to be her daughter—how it meant that nothing would get in my way. I wouldn't let my time in Hollywood (Florida) break me. I decided you need the failure to earn the triumph. The failure is what shows you that art is not just an impulse but a practice that takes time and patience and humility. You do it wrong so you can learn it right. And by the time we got to the airport I decided that *Nose Job* would be the story I'd tell people about how bad things got before they got good.

Going Downtown

NYU's curriculum was designed so that, during your time there, you'd have to perform every role on a film set, from producer to sound engineer. It's what attracted me to the school in the first place, and while those are all roles every director should know, I feel a lot of guilt for all the destruction I caused.

I'm a danger on set (and, arguably, in life) when not directing. As the second AC (assistant camera person, responsible for loading the Super 16 film), I failed to lock the film magazine correctly, which exposed the roll to the light and rendered a good chunk of the day's shoot completely worthless. As the script supervisor, I was in charge of keeping track of everything that happened during a take for the sake of continuity in the edit, from ad-libbed lines to who had hair tucked behind what ear, but with my ADHD I could barely keep track of what scene we were on, let alone which hand the actor's coffee cup was in. As a boom operator, I somehow managed to point the microphone upside down, so it picked up all of the ceiling fan and none of the dialogue. I'm honestly just grateful I didn't hurt anybody.

Eventually, I discovered I was a decent assistant director. The AD is responsible for keeping the day moving, bossing people around without making them feel bullied, and having absolutely no contact with any equipment. The best part about ADing is that you spend a great deal of your day strategizing in the inner circle with the director and the cinematographer. Even though we were all classmates, and I'd seen each of them in various states of desperate, pathetic, and vulnerable, the moment anyone took on the role of director or cinematographer, they transformed into a minor god in my eyes. That's just the way it is when you start living most of your waking hours on a film set: you bow down to the hierarchy. You tell yourself that the hierarchy is what enables the machine to move (even though it can often be what keeps the environment toxic and full of damaged, power-hungry egomaniacs, but I digress).

During one of my many stints as an AD, I got the hots for this cinematographer who kinda reminded me of Jughead from the *Archie* comics, which I'd been obsessed with as a girl (and am only now realizing is most likely the root of my penchant for gangly uninterested men with freakishly high metabolisms). I realized I had the hots for him as we were fleeing the Staten Island home of an extremely angry seventy-four-year-old Albanian woman who'd just discovered two tiny chunks of paint chipped off her wall. The chipped paint was 100 percent my fault (sorry, Blerta), as I was the one who'd hastily yanked off the wallpaper that the art department had taped up (and requested I not touch). I was rushing us out of there because we were trying to escape a snowstorm that was well underway and had already piled up six inches of snow. Once we'd packed my dad's Honda Civic with people and equipment, I drove exactly five feet before the wheels got stuck. Which is how I found myself pushing the car down the street with Jughead, completely delirious from exhaustion and laughing so hard my sides ached

as my skirt inched its way up my thighs and my tights ran in
the opposite direction, because of course that was the day I'd
dressed up to play an extra when we couldn't find enough
Albanian-looking faces on Craigslist.

A few nights later, we wrapped the shoot. Jughead and I
shared a cab to Brooklyn, and I kissed him after he helped me
hoist my things out of the trunk. He accepted my kiss for a
polite amount of time, then got back in the cab, which drove off
while I contemplated how many first kisses the poor cab driver
had been forced to witness throughout his career.

It wasn't a great kiss. If the kissing isn't right from the
start, you're fucked. I keep learning and forgetting this lesson
over and over through the course of my life. Jughead and I
shared mutual respect, crippling self-disgust laced with ambition, and not much else, but I kept trying to turn it into ro-
mance. This led to a six-month game of cat and mouse, where
I'd chase him down and dull his defenses with attention and
alcohol, and we'd wind up in bed: ashamed, unsatisfied, and
promising it would never happen again.

I'd be on the brink of deleting his number, and then I'd
catch him looking at me in a way that felt like love but was
most likely the look of a man doing mental math. My crush
persisted because sprinkled through his apathy were sporadic
moments of connection and fun, and I so desperately craved a
distraction from the never-ending panic attack that was being
a grad student.

The school years were bookended with epic sweaty dance
parties that went down in the cramped common space on the
tenth floor of the Tisch building. The couches would be pushed
up against a wall and the coffee tables stored in an editing
suite, and an endless supply of Brooklyn Lager and cheap
vodka flowed. These parties, one in September and one in May,
bound us together through the nonstop cycle of anxiety, dick-

measuring, and failure. We drank hard, we danced hard, and it felt good to be part of something.

My whole life changed at one of those parties, at the end of my second year. I was in it to win it with the tequila that night, clutching a plastic water bottle I'd filled with it to my chest. Why I chose not to use a cup I have absolutely no idea; fewer trips to the bar, I guess? I'd just spotted Jughead and was half-hiding/full-spying, trying to gauge his level of intoxication. Then, as I was planning my opening line between swigs of water bottle tequila, I walked straight SMACK into the woman who would free me from everything I hated about my life at that moment.

I burst into a desperate apology, which led into a gratu-itously detailed explanation for why I'd bumped into her, and then even *more* unnecessary oversharing, and in a matter of minutes Jughead went from mild obsession to punch line. It was like a spell had broken. I was undone by her generous, full-face laughs. The words came tumbling out of my mouth: a play-by-play of me, Jughead, and my shitty second-year film, all my cards laid before this woman whose name I'd only just learned.

It was Ingrid, which struck me as a bit exotic and weirdly old-fashioned and perfectly suited to her. She was older, but in the year below me. I'd seen her once before and registered her as a lesbian, but she was just an extra then. Now she was the star. I wondered, *Who is this creature who doesn't seem to give a shit about any of the status symbols that every other person at NYU lives by?**

---

* Things like: tracking the success of every other person in the room, never not wearing a leather jacket, having a close personal "friendship" with James Franco, and making the kind of work that was favored among the faculty (which was usually a father/son coming-of-age story where Daddy drinks and they're on a road trip).

We made out fast and hard in the smokers' nook outside the front entrance. It wasn't until we were in the cab on our way to my place that I realized I was definitely, no question, going to vomit. The next thing I knew I was crouched over on Houston Street while cars whizzed by so fast they felt like slaps to my ears. Ingrid got me home, put me to bed, and even found a tiny trash can she placed by my head, along with a glass of water.

I woke up with that specific brand of mortification exclusive to binge drinking. I had to do some digging to track down her email address, and when I finally did, I spat out a clumsy apology that used eight times more exclamation points than necessary and asked if I could take her out to dinner.

I biked to the restaurant from Tisch that Friday, impulsively stopping at the Sephora in Soho on the way to slap on tester foundation to mask my raging cystic acne, which covered every inch of real estate on my cheeks at that time. Then, I sweated it all off somewhere on the Manhattan Bridge. I wasn't sure if it was a date or a hang, but I was hopeful.

The moment we locked eyes I knew it was a date. It was her smile that told me. She'd known it was a date when she'd arrived, on time, ten minutes earlier, and there was a reservation for us under my name. It was one of those dinners where one story bleeds into another and no train of thought reaches a conclusion, it just opens up into new branches. We were instant playmates. It didn't matter that I wasn't cool or popular or "one to watch." And, unlike with Jughead, nothing was too cringe or too much information. She wanted all the information and more.

I was nearing the end of my time at Renfrew when we met, so when she asked me about my days, I didn't hold back. I told her I'd spent a good bulk of my time in various forms of group therapy in rooms full of anorexics, bulimics, and binge eaters, to which she replied, "Tell me more." It felt revolutionary. I'm pretty sure if I'd said the word *binge* to Jughead his beard would have instantly spread up over the top half of his face and swallowed him whole.

It seemed too good to be true. Up until that point, there'd always been a lingering fear gnawing away at me, whispering into my ear, *What if you're not actually gay?* I'd been with women. I knew I was attracted to women. But I still hadn't been "downtown," if you know what I mean. Not even with Nisha. Going downtown felt like a big, defining moment. If you go downtown and you're into it, then there's no denying you're a legit homosexual. Even if you're attracted to men as well, a lady capable of downtown fun time with another lady is gay. I decided that before someone went downtown, they really couldn't know if they were gay, and it scared the shit out of me. I was crazy about Ingrid from the second we'd met, but what if I was just enamored with a new friend? Had I turned it sexual because of my desperate need for validation? There was only one way to find out for sure.

I went downtown and angels sang. I went downtown and all my doubts melted away. I went downtown, and it was like coming home.

It was easy to love Ingrid. She was kind, charming, sexy, and unpretentious. She was raised outside Orlando by a born-again Jehovah's Witness. We'd both known fear young. Her wounds were different from mine, deeper, but she was the first person I'd met who understood the very specific brand of coming-of-age hurt I'd been lugging around: razor-sharp and still throbbing. We fit. I didn't have to make edits while her back was turned. Even when we went to the Met, we took the same amount of time to stroll through each exhibit, and it struck me as the most romantic test of compatibility ever devised.

She had a past. She'd loved so many women, I had to write down their names to remember them all. Women she'd had different lives with, in different haircuts and different states. One down south with whom she'd adopted a husky, Zeke. Months earlier, I'd written down a list of things I wanted in a romantic partner, and one of them was "someone with a big dog." It felt like I'd wished her into existence. I was convinced that it was forever and that the names from her past were the building blocks to arriving at us.

A few months into our relationship, I began my last year of film school, where I began studying under the filmmaker Ira Sachs. Just like his films, Ira is sensitive, thoughtful, intelligent, and precise. He was the best directing teacher I'd ever had, and all the students in that class ended up producing their strongest work. What made him great was that he never tried to teach us how to direct. To pretend that there's a right and a wrong way to do it is to not understand the job. There's no one-size-fits-all protocol. You have to discover what works for you through trial and error, and while you stumble into learning your own pace, style, and language, you need to remain inspired and in awe of the practice itself, which is exactly what he showed us in that class.

Over the course of the semester, Ira shared the work of the auteurs he loved and gave us one assignment: make a short film and screen it at the end of the semester. It could be any length, any subject matter, any style. You could workshop it in class or keep it a secret until the screening. The only rule was you had to screen *something*.

By that point, my commitment to school had taken a back seat to Ingrid. I lost myself to the joy of being hers. She lived in Park Slope, a family-friendly lesbian mecca in Brooklyn. We loved every inch of that neighborhood: from the intensity of the Israeli product boycott politics at the food co-op, to the dirty-diaper stench of the Tea Lounge, a massive coffee shop/bar/ performance space that hosted daily Mommy and Me sing-alongs. We biked everywhere, made our own granola, wore our sports bras when not sporty, and essentially became walking clichés of the place. That said, there was a weird tension between our gayness and the alienation we felt within the gay world at large.

I was newly out of the closet and desperate to adopt gay culture as my own, but when I looked around, I couldn't see myself in it. Pride felt like a rainbow-hued k-hole nightmare. The lesbians I knew were into team sports like rugby or softball. I, on the other hand, had no athletic abilities, felt victimized merely pushing my way onto the subway, and had lasted exactly ten minutes into rugby team tryouts. Cinema was my preferred entryway into any new world, but all the gay films I knew of at that point were melodramatic, cheesy, and somehow both neutered and bordering on soft-core porn.* For someone having such a sexy time being gay, the *brand* of being gay was feeling deeply unsexy.

Meanwhile, Ingrid was sorting through her own similar discomfort, and, as a result of our mutual coming-of-gay crisis, we mercilessly skewered all things queer like snarky teenagers at a family cookout. We were superficial, homophobic lesbians, and it welded us to each other. One day, while I was waxing poetic about my deep discomfort with lesbian brides who both opt to wear gowns,† Ingrid said, "This should be your film for Ira's class. This conversation, and what assholes we are!"

---

* I had yet to see *High Art, Water Lilies, Show Me Love, Bound, Desert Hearts, D.E.B.S., Personal Best, Watermelon Woman, Go Fish, But I'm a Cheerleader,* or any of the other incredible lesbian films that I would have found if I'd put in the slightest bit more effort instead of complaining.

† I had a lot of internalized homophobia to unpack.

We were obsessed with *Louie* and *Curb Your Enthusiasm*. We wanted to lampoon our worst prejudices and paranoias while calling out the absurdity of the world around us, just like they did. We quickly threw together a script, creating exaggerated alter egos of ourselves. Then we went to the park and filmed for a few hours before class. There were no actors and no big crew, just the two of us and a friend filming in exchange for lunch. That night, we edited it together, passing the laptop back and forth. It was so easy: no auditions, no overthinking, no lights, no big locations, just the two of us trying shit out and having fun. It was an exercise in saying yes to every first instinct. Ingrid had all my trust, so when she said a joke worked, it worked. I never worried about whether another director would have approved the frame because no other director would have considered making anything like this. It was singular to the two of us.

When we screened it at Ira's end of semester screening, the feeling in the room was unlike anything I'd experienced up until that point. Every joke killed. The audience was on board for each second of it, and by the end you could feel their hunger for more. It was the best feeling I'd ever known. Afterward, people looked at me with newfound respect, like they'd finally figured me out. I felt like I'd finally figured me out too.

High off the approval, we made another short film, and then another, and started posting them online. We were inspired by *Thunderant*, Fred Armisen and Carrie Brownstein's precursor to *Portlandia*. It was 2011, and the concept of putting original content on the web felt daring and hadn't really been explored much up until that point, so we decided we were making a web series, which literally meant nothing, because there was no such thing at the time. We called it *The Slope* and kept shooting an "episode" a week. We built the story of each episode around whatever Park Slope location we had access to and cast whatever friend agreed to give us their time. Since a web series was a brand-new format that hadn't existed before that moment, it didn't feel like there was a right or wrong way to proceed. We just made it up as we went along.

The show stemmed from the insecurity that we weren't the "right" kind of gay, and by putting it out there we realized there were so many people who felt the exact same way. Each week our audience grew, until eventually we started getting press and invitations to screen around the world, and *then* the holy grail of student filmmaker aspirations: a spot in *Filmmaker* magazine's 25 New Faces of Film. Getting on that list gave me the confidence to start calling myself a filmmaker, and from then on I made it so.

Before *The Slope*, the experience of making films felt futile, like swimming against the tide. I kept struggling to follow rules that made no sense to me. I was twenty-six, and I'd spent my whole life obediently following rules: my parents', my teachers', even Wong Kar Wai's. Having the audacity to love another woman changed everything. It connected me to my own instincts, and it gave me courage to cut free from all the outside voices in my head. Knowing and loving Ingrid specifically—funny, sharp, fearless, and unapologetic—introduced me to my own.

"Being the Homophobia"

I was nineteen, sitting with my parents and their friends at a restaurant when Taraneh—the one who prides herself on getting the party started, and generally "going there"—announced, "Honestly, I would rather my kids have cancer than to be gay." She laughed, "They tell me, 'Mommy! You are being the homophobia,' but it's true!"

Another woman at the table shared an anecdote about the gay colorist at her hair salon and how she was cool with him touching her hair. The conversation evolved into people's relationships with their colorists, general salon frustrations, and the optimal blond-to-chestnut color ratio. You know, the banal chitchat of ladies who are waiting for the mimosas to arrive and may not actually like one another but have been forced into friendship because they're the only human beings who share the same language, food, and history within a five-hundred-mile radius.

My mom dug her fingers into my right thigh while I stared down at my shorts and watched the denim suck up tears. "I'd rather my kids have cancer than be gay." I didn't want my face to betray me, but I didn't know how to shape it into something neutral, so I kept it down. I couldn't tell if my mom's tight grip on me said, *I'm sorry* or *Don't you dare open your mouth.*

Every adult at the table that day expected their child to marry an Iranian, specifically one whose parents they knew and loved. It was what each of them had done for their own parents. Didn't they deserve the same courtesy? We all knew that Taraneh's son had an American girlfriend and that she saw the girl as something he was getting out of his system before settling down. And of course he eventually did break up with her and marry the niece of one of the other women at that table. It was what was expected of him.

The Little Mermaid came out when I was five years old, and when I saw it, I believed it to be a work of genius. My mother did not agree. She didn't love that Ariel disobeys her father to chase after some guy and ends up putting her entire species at risk. There's one scene she *really* hated, where Ariel screams, "I'M SIXTEEN YEARS OLD, I'M NOT A CHILD!" My mother couldn't stomach that kind of insolence and took every opportunity to remind me that Ariel was the ungrateful, spoiled product of the very worst of American culture. She told me to be like Belle from *Beauty and the Beast*. In case you missed it, Belle risks her life to replace her father as prisoner to a bloodthirsty beast, which remains the base level of sacrifice expected of you as the child of immigrants.

I told my parents I was in love with a woman six years after that weekend upstate with Taraneh. I did it with my eyes closed, like I was jumping off a skyscraper. I was standing in the kitchen I grew up in. I can still remember the feeling in my stomach: all the weight and no weight, like the worst roller-coaster drop imaginable. It's the feeling of shame and guilt head-butting each other.

When my mom's upset, she wants all the information: Who is she? Where is she? When did you? Where did you? Like she's a bad news detective, scanning for lies and cover-ups, trying to sniff out the even bigger betrayal you're hiding behind your back. My father's the opposite. He retreats. You can tell it's bad when he goes completely silent. It was like I'd flipped his "off" switch. He betrayed nothing, said nothing. If you're really going for the jugular, muteness is the ultimate power move. There's no way to counter.

My brother, Ardavan, wanted to know what the fuck was wrong with me: "Why can't you keep your private life private?" Sometimes it feels like he's my third, least approving parent. Growing up, he took it upon himself to cover my eyes during the sex scenes at the movies. He was born in Iran, five years before me. They left the country when he was forty days old.* He may have only lived there a little over a month, but it was enough to infuse him with an Iranian-ness that's always eluded me.

I was born in New York, which is why I'm an entitled millennial cliché. "Keep[ing] your private life private" didn't feel like an option. I'm incapable of lying, and it's a character flaw. It's gauche to be so straightforward. There's no elegance, no subtlety in it. When you're talking to an Iranian, the truth is nebulous. It bends and stretches to find a new shape.

Iranians communicate their meaning in the spaces between the words. The implications. You have to learn a second, unspoken dialogue. There's even a word for it, *tarof*, which is the art of disingenuous generosity. We're raised to keep offering things we don't actually want to offer, and say things we don't actually mean but must say out of mandatory, aggressive po-

* Fun fact: Mom smuggled her diamonds out in his diapers.

liteness. If you compliment someone on something they own, they'll automatically offer it to you:

"Nice hat."

"It's yours!"

But no offer is legitimate until it's been extended a minimum of three times.

When you go to pay for something at the bazaar, they'll say, "For you, it's free! You're like a sister/daughter/mother to me, I could never charge you!" Then you have to convince them to charge you for it. And *then* you have to haggle the price down to something reasonable.

I'm a bad Persian. I'm too honest, and I'm too horny. Not to brag, but my Barbies and I invented sixty-nining. My single Ken serviced an army of insatiable identical blondes. And when Ken couldn't handle the task, Totally Hair Barbie would step in. Something was definitely up with me. I used to lie in bed and fall asleep to thoughts of Yasmine Bleeth playing beach volleyball in slow motion.

I knew to be ashamed. There was a strict, unspoken code of conduct at home, and one of the rules was that we didn't acknowledge the existence of sex. When I was twelve, my mother called me into her room. I could tell I'd done something wrong. "Ardavan said there's a box of tampons on top of your dresser, where anyone could see. You can't leave that kind of thing out in the open. It's ugly."

Let's break this down: My seventeen-year-old brother had walked past my room and spotted an unopened box of Playtex Gentle Glides. Then he decided the appropriate response would be to complain to our mother about the sheer audacity of someone leaving a box of Playtex Gentle Glides out in broad daylight. My mother, in turn, heard his complaint, considered it valid, and reprimanded me. This was the level of formality in the house I grew up in. It felt like we belonged, not only to different generations but to different dimensions. It felt like every impulse I had was the wrong one.

Around the time I started feeling hot for Yasmine Bleeth, a picture book materialized among my toys, seemingly out of nowhere. My parents must have smelled it on me. "Where Did I Come From?" asked huge black letters against a white background with a fat cartoon baby peeking out at you from the "o" in "from." It was a straightforward explanation of sex for children (where the illustrator made everyone a little bit fat, which I appreciate). What was weird about the book's presence in my life was that it arrived with absolutely no dialogue whatsoever. At one point, I gathered all my courage and straight-up asked, "Where do babies come from?" To which my mother replied, "Read the book." End of discussion.

I knew what sex was, but I didn't know much else. I thought kissing with tongue was something women weren't allowed to do with anyone other than their husbands, by law. I learned about masturbation at eleven when a classmate informed me that instead of simply watching *Curly Sue* and eating too much popcorn at sleepovers like I did, the boys in our class would masturbate in front of each other. I remember my whole worldview shifting as I realized sex was a thing that unmarried people engaged in outside of Barbie make-believe playtime. But even once I knew about the existence of masturbation, I assumed only boys could do it, until eleventh grade, when I overheard Lindsay Jones referencing her own masturbation practices. I remember staring at her in shock, unsure of how that was even possible. She had to explain what the clitoris was. I was sixteen, and my classmates were fucking, but I didn't even know I was capable of jerking off.

There was no precedent for being gay and Iranian. None of us had ever even *heard* of a gay Iranian. Claiming it for myself felt ridiculous, like coming out as a leprechaun. In fact, around that time the Iranian president, Mahmoud Ahmadinejad, publicly announced, "In Iran, we don't have homosexuals." He failed to mention that might have something to do with the fact that, in Iran, homosexuality is punishable by death.

I took my steps blind. After I came out, my parents and I didn't talk much for about a year and a half. Dad remained silent, while my mom tried. We engaged in a very public teary whisper fight on the fourth floor of MoMA. She even met Ingrid and me for the most uncomfortable bowl of soup of my life at Le Pain Quotidien. But it was no good. I'd done the unspeakable: I'd cut the immigrant child umbilical cord, the one held together with complete and utter obedience. At what point does your life get to be yours and not your parents' or your community's? I was raised to believe that the answer was never.

To add insult to injury, I wasn't even saying I was fully gay: I came out as bisexual, which begs the question: What the fuck is your problem? I knew I was capable of finding love with a man. I could have decided to ignore the part of me that was attracted to women. "If you have the choice, why would you choose this?" my mother wanted to know.

Some would argue that being gay isn't a choice, but for me it was. I'm not talking about attraction—who you love and lust after is sewn into your being. By "choice," I'm referring to the actions I took. It's a choice to put your needs over your culture's demands. I've watched plenty of people ignore their desires for the sake of their family. I chose to pursue the instant attraction I felt for Ingrid, even though I knew it would not only humiliate my family but break their hearts.

So, why did I choose it?

Uh . . . I dunno. Because I want to have my cake and eat it too? Because the last guy I'd slept with left me cold, but Ingrid could look beyond the cystic acne?

Maybe it's because I'm a selfish American shithead. Maybe it's because I saw what living according to the rules did to my parents, and I didn't want that for myself. And maybe I was tired of living in fear of what Mommy and Daddy would disapprove of. Mostly I think it was because Renfrew had changed me. It had showed me how my shame had made me sick, and I didn't want to be sick anymore.

Ingrid and I broke up during the height of our success with *The Slope*, and it wasn't pretty. We wanted opposite things out of a relationship and needed space to let go of each other, but each week a new professional opportunity would fall into our laps. The longer we held on to each other and the show, the uglier and more below-the-belt our fights got. I became a complete mess. I'm talking hysterical sobbing on the subway and cornering an acquaintance you barely know to tell them your side of the story kinda mess. One Saturday, my parents offered to drive me to her place so I could pick up the last of my things, and I, being too pathetic to hold up my end of my estrangement from them, agreed.

It was surreal, directing my father to Ingrid's apartment, the place where I'd lived the life they refused to know anything about. It felt taboo, like we were on a family outing to a torture dungeon. They sat in the car and watched me unlock her door as I let myself in for the last time. Minutes later, I closed it, carrying a shoebox filled with the last traces of me in her home. I stepped into my parents' car and proceeded to cry so hard I could barely breathe. Nobody said anything for about a mile. Then my dad spoke.

"Desi. That was puppy love."

Oh, my heart. My heart ached and swelled at once. He'd said "love." He'd given my loss dignity, while offering me hope for something better. It was the exact moment I understood the meaning of unconditional love. I'd had to test it to feel its shape. As soon as he said it I knew that I was still his kid, despite his contempt for my choices. I knew that eventually we'd be okay.

Coming out was the hardest, smartest thing I've ever done. There was no way to know if they'd ever get over their own rules of living and bend to accept the ones I was establishing for myself, especially when there was no precedent for establishing your own rules in our family. Once I'd done it, I felt invincible. Do you know what's scary after destroying the hopes and dreams of the people who created you? Literally nothing. It was the exact moment my adult life began.

I once heard my father say, "I knew I only had two choices: get over it or lose my child." I had faced a similar choice: live life on my own terms and risk losing my family, or live according to their rules and never get the opportunity to meet myself. I took a calculated risk, and against all odds, I won.

My First Movie

From the moment I understood that movies were a thing that people could actually write and direct and author, I knew that it was the language I needed to be speaking. When I toured the facilities at NYU on the day of my grad school interview, the first thing I asked my student guide was "Can you make a feature for your thesis?"

"Sure, if you can raise the money."

"Are YOU going to make a feature for your thesis?"

"Probably not, I don't feel ready."

It was a reasonable reply to an invasive question, but all I could think was *I was born ready, motherfucker.*

Three years later the time came to shoot my thesis, and *The Slope* was gaining traction. Every week, our viewership grew, more positive press came out, and exciting opportunities were falling into our laps. Meanwhile, my relationship with Ingrid was intolerable. Neither one of us was willing to give up on our baby after our breakup, so we kept shooting episodes, but as our relationship atrophied, so did our ability to exist in the same space. Finally Ingrid quit.

She (wisely) drew a boundary and informed me that she could "no longer profit off of our failed relationship." The line stuck with me because all I could think at that moment was *I'd better fucking profit off of it. I'd better take this heartache and turn it into something useful—something to make up for the fact that the only person in the world who saw me as funny and fearless and fuckable now looks at me with so much disdain it hits like a sucker punch.* My determination to keep pushing forward with the show no matter how horrible our dynamic became took on a manic quality. I couldn't let go.

The Slope had made it okay for me to be gay, okay to be an outsider, okay to have my own particular sense of humor (which tends to lean into the dark and absurd in a way that works well on-screen but can be off-putting in life). It was my first taste of popularity, and it had transformed the two of us into minor celebrities at school. I remember walking down the halls thinking, *Oh*, this *is what it feels like when people think you're talented.* Then we broke up and the show ended. But even though the door to our relationship had closed, the window of opportunity we'd created for ourselves was still cracked open. So as Ingrid and I stopped talking, I started writing my first movie.

What made the web series work was that it was simple to shoot and played to our strengths, so I mapped out the feature with those elements in mind. I wrote for locations I had access to, actors I knew personally, and arguments I'd had recently. Since I'd never shaped a narrative longer than twenty pages, I lifted the structure of Bergman's *Scenes from a Marriage*, which tracks one couple over six long scenes as their relationship changes over the course of a decade. The script I wrote had twelve scenes and tracked a relationship over the course of one year. I figured I could shoot a scene a month, editing and fundraising as I went.

I sped through a draft and shared it with Cecilia to get her thoughts. Every six months one of us would fly out to visit the other in either New York or London, and around the time I started grad school at NYU, she began pursuing a master in film production at Westminster University. She read my script and offered to produce it, and it was, hands down, the best offer of my life. She wanted to help me transform what I'd written into something more ambitious than my twelve-scene/twelve-month concept. Her idea was to make the film about the girl, not the couple: a heartbroken, closeted girl from an Iranian family. She threw me a lifeline that allowed me to stop trying to build something from the wreckage of my web series and move on with my life. I said yes and was immediately hit with a wave of relief. I wasn't on my own anymore. I was going to do this with my friend—my friend who is so much smarter than me!

I've been writing scripts since I was nine and wrote that sketch for "Vomlet: The Omelet Made of Vomit!" I've always had a voice, but when Cecilia and I started working together, she refined it. From the start, she displayed a gift for curating my life and personality into a scene, a story, and a genre. I'd throw all my thoughts and stories and ideas in her general direction, and she'd pluck out the gems, then help form them into something bigger, better, and somewhat coherent. Neither one of us had any idea what we were doing, so we made up the rules as we went along.

She gave me assignments. She asked me to write scenes inspired by the aspects of my life she found interesting. The elements that she gravitated toward tended to be the ones that had made me stand out as a freak throughout life: my sexuality, my race, and my humor. She lovingly laughed at my foibles. She knew me and my stories inside and out, and milked them for material like she was playing an instrument: "Remember that time when you told the saleslady at Bra Smyth every last detail of your sexual history before spending rent money on thickly padded bras you thought would transform your love life? And the minute you got home you realized they made you look like you'd stuffed traffic cones down your shirt? Remember how you had the exact same experience two weeks later with the lady at Lush? And then the lady at that vitamin store?" She gleaned the memories, and I wrote the scenes.

We spent a year rewriting and fundraising while I did short stints of being a live-in nanny to Arab billionaires and teaching filmmaking to five-year-olds. During that year I was rejected by every single grant and lab I applied to. One female-filmmaker grant hated the script so much they advised us to give up on it completely. A series of rejection letters arrived back-to-back one week in December, and it felt like we were the only two people in the world who thought making the film was a good idea.

But not making the film was never an option. There was no plan B. Perhaps the key ingredient to becoming a filmmaker is having no other skills, talent, or interests, and being enough of an egomaniac to persist when all the odds are stacked against you. What I'd come to learn in the following decade is that the odds are *always* stacked against you. It turns out that, when it comes to making movies, "This is impossible and I should give up" is a storm cloud hanging over your head for about 75 percent of the process.

In the summer of 2013, Cecilia and her business partner, Olivier Kaempfer, came through with the budget, and we went into production on *Appropriate Behavior*. We had $200,000 to work with—more money than I'd ever dreamed of shooting a

film with, and yet, I'd come to learn, no money at all in the
world of filmmaking, a budget so tiny they call it micro. Working with a microbudget means constant compromise and making the last option the best option. For me, this was an ideal
approach to facing the gargantuan task of shooting my first
film. It ended up eliciting the same brand of calm creative flow
I slip into when figuring out how to make a meal out of whatever's left in the fridge. I cannot speak more highly of the
"fridge leftover" approach to filmmaking. First you ask yourself, "What do I have at my disposal?" Then you take stock of
who and what's around you. Then figure out what's most important and utilize what you've got to fit those needs.

There's an interview with director Catherine Breillat in the
Criterion Collection edition of her film *Fat Girl** where she
says, "I don't make the film, I am the film." Her words stayed
with me from the moment I first heard them, but I didn't really
get what they meant until I was on my first feature film set as
a director. Then it made sense. You can't really know what directing is until you do it. Every single director has a different
definition of it, but here's mine: directing is figuring out the
love language of each person on set. It's knowing when to cre-
scendo and let the art department go crazy on a location, and
when to turn down the volume so every scene doesn't look like
it takes place during a fever dream, which would definitely be
cool but might not be in service of your story, and the story is
KING. It's your responsibility to protect it. You don't make the
film; your cast and crew make the film. You *are* the film. You're
the only person with the full blueprint in your head. How you
choose to communicate that blueprint is contingent on who you
are and what you want to make.

I learned what directing was on the set of *Appropriate Be-*

---

* One of the best coming-of-age films of all time.

havior. I didn't necessarily do it well, but I discovered what it entailed in a way that film school hadn't prepared me for. A lot of directing is people-reading. Some of your collaborators will crave constant hand-holding, while others will want free rein. Then there's a third category: the ones you have to trick into thinking you've left them to their own devices, when in actuality they're clutching onto a steering wheel attached to nothing. In the meantime, while all of that's happening, you're keeping a sharp eye on the footage you've shot, the footage you need, and the footage you're getting right this very second. It's all systems go, all at once, and I've never felt more alive, more joyful, more *myself* than when I'm doing this job and doing it well.

Directing is having all the ego and none of it: the ego to hypnotize people into believing in your vision, while often swallowing it back to allow someone else's ego to run wild in order for them to do their best work. Nine times out of ten, that person will be an actor, and that is only because acting can be the most vulnerable and disempowering position on set. Nobody ever considers this because sets are a hierarchy and actors sit at the top of the pecking order, but it can be incredibly lonely at the top. Your face and your body belong to the film for the duration of the shoot, and every time you're doing your job, everyone is watching you find your footing, make mistakes, and throw paint at the wall. You can't take a shit without at least three different department heads knowing about it, and I know this because I was the star of my first movie and learned all these lessons the hard way.

Writing the script for myself to star in felt like a no-brainer. Ingrid and I had starred in *The Slope*, so I was in the habit of writing for myself, and the idea of casting a hotter version of me to do an impression felt antiseptic. I wanted to put my money where my mouth was. Besides high school plays and acting classes, I had no experience, but was confident I could do it because . . . why not? I went into the shoot wildly naive. I had no idea how difficult it would be to act or direct, let alone do both jobs at once.

To act is to be deeply rooted in the moment you're filming, while also cognizant of the moment that comes before in the script, the moment that comes next, and how they all fit within the narrative of your character's arc over the course of the film. You have to keep all of that at the forefront of your mind while remaining raw, open, and flexible enough to bend with the scene and be present with your scene partner as it plays out in real time. Then you might have to completely change gears according to the notes you're given between each take. Meanwhile, you can't miss a step in the choreography of the dance you're locked into with the camera, light, and continuity. If you make one mistake and fail to pick up your bag with your right hand during the third line of your second speech, the majority of that take might be unusable. Sometimes when I'm acting, the moment I hear ACTION, all I can think is *YOU'RE FUCKING IT UP! YOU'RE NOT IN THE SCENE. YOU'RE UP HERE WITH ME, THE WORST THOUGHTS IN YOUR HEAD, FUCKING IT UP!*

Acting while directing means always half-assing half your job. The two roles aren't compatible: if directing is knowing all the answers, acting is asking all the questions. To direct is to open yourself up to everything and everyone on set, while acting often means shutting down your awareness of the rest of the world so you can lose yourself to the fictional reality of the film. To do both at once feels like an attempt at being both parent and child simultaneously. An actor has to jump, trusting they'll be caught, while the director assembles the harness beneath.

Meanwhile it's the *producer* who's laid their own body flat underneath in case the harness breaks. While I was struggling to be both parent and child, Cecilia was the person who kept the film afloat. There's a scene where my character has a threesome that goes awry. After we shot the first take, I watched playback on a tiny monitor. Midway through the footage, I stopped watching and began to focus my energy on relaxing the muscles on my face so that it revealed absolutely nothing. I have one of those faces you can see right through, and I didn't want my crew and scene partners (the incredible Robyn Rikoon and Christopher James Baker) to know that I was freaking the fuck out. The seconds crawled by as I battled a completely silent, poker-faced panic attack. When the take was through, I excused myself to the bathroom and locked the door behind me.

In the bathroom, I pulled my knees up to my chest, tightening into a ball, and thought, *FUCK FUCK FUCK FUCK FUCK FUCK FUCK FUCK FUCK FUCK FUCK FUCK FUCK FUCK FUCK FUCK FUCK FUCK FUCK FUCK FUCK FUCK FUCK FUCK FUCK FUCK FUCK FUCK FUCK FUCK FUCK FUCK FUCK FUCK FUCK FUCK FUCK FUCK FUCK FUCK FUCK FUCK FUCK FUCK FUCK FUCK FUCK FUCK FUCK FUCK FUCK FUCK FUCK FUCK FUCK FUCK FUCK FUCK FUCK FUCK FUCK FUCK FUCK FUCK FUCK FUCK FUCK FUCK FUCK FUCK FUCK FUCK FUCK FUCK FUCK FUCK FUCK FUCK FUCK FUCK FUCK FUCK FUCK FUCK FUCK FUCK FUCK FUCK FUCK FUCK FUCK FUCK FUCK FUCK FUCK FUCK*.

Then there was a knock at the door.

"It's me."

I let Cecilia in.

"It looks like porn!" I told her. "It's gratuitous and humiliating and we have to shut this down!"

I started pitching new dialogue, new blocking, some kind of escape route to get us out of the mess I'd created. To my shock, she looked at me with a calm, easy confidence I'd never seen in her before and said, "It's good. Trust me, it's good."

Cecilia and I communicate mostly in *30 Rock* quotes. Now, crouching next to me in the bathroom, she reminded me of the episode where Liz Lemon gets her own talk show, and being on camera messes with her perspective so drastically that she transforms into a nervous wreck, resulting in three horrible haircuts and an off-brand laser eye surgery that makes her cry out of her mouth. Then she locks herself in her dressing room and battles it out in the mirror: Actor Liz versus Producer Liz. The same thing was happening to me: Actor Desiree was so uncomfortable seeing herself in the threesome sex scene that she convinced Director Desiree the whole thing needed to be rewritten into a scene where they play Monopoly instead. Cecilia reminded me that between the two of us, she's always been the prude, so if she didn't think the scene was crossing a line, I had to go ahead and accept that I might be biased. And with that, Cecilia unlocked the bathroom door. I took my clothes off, got back on my knees, and simulated oral sex in front of my colleagues like the boss I am.

To this day, that threesome scene remains the best thing I've ever filmed. It's the rare example of the execution not just aligning with my intention but surpassing it to create a moment that's more funny, evocative, and raw than I'd imagined it could be. I couldn't see it in real time because I was too vulnerable, but Cecilia guided me through the discomfort, and that's how I survived the shoot.

Ten days after we'd wrapped principal photography, I watched an assembly of the movie and wrote Cecilia the following email:

Hi,

I watched the cut and . . . I know first cuts can be rough to watch, but I just don't see how this is going to be a movie.

Oh man, it's bad. So bad. It made no sense. I'm a hack. I cannot believe this script seemed like something to film. On the way home it hit me that this may be the time to give up on wanting to support myself making movies and writing and being a creative, self-indulgent camera-whore. Like, maybe I'm not one of the lucky ones who gets to live her dream & why did I feel entitled to do that in the first place? Adults grow the fuck up and get real jobs.

I love you and the fact that you were creatively involved is its one saving grace.

xoxo Desi

Shooting your film is getting high off the pace of it, which fuels decisiveness and a clarity of vision. The ticking clock becomes the villain you battle each day, against all odds, to come out victorious. You head home from set thinking, *You did it! You made your day!* Exactly *what* did you make? Who knows! Whatever it was, it felt right in the moment and YOU ARE A ROCKSTAR!*

Editing your film is swimming in your mistakes as time slows down, your confidence dwindles, and your caloric intake skyrockets. It's the puberty portion of the process, and it is *not* pretty. The film is no longer idealized potential that lives in your head. It's tangible, and the pieces of it have been assembled into the worst Frankenstein version of itself. You stare at the same footage over and over like it's a Magic Eye poster you can't solve. You watch and brainstorm and give up, and then gain a burst of energy around 1 A.M. when you start penning voiceover that you're convinced will fix the film. Then you de-

---

* Also you haven't slept more than three hours in three weeks, suddenly you're a smoker, and dinner was a fistful of gummy bears.

lete the whole thing the next day because your editor failed to jump up and down and scream, "YOU'RE A GENIUS!" when you showed it to her.

My editor was the brilliant Sara Shaw, an NYU classmate and one of the sharpest, most painfully critical minds I know. Having her as a collaborator throughout my career has been one of the greatest tools in my arsenal, but back then, neither one of us had worked on a feature, so it was the blind leading the blind. Her taste is impeccable, which means her standards were far too high. We weren't experienced enough to know how to tolerate sitting through so much shitty footage.

We slogged through the miserable process, inching our way forward for months until, ever so slowly, solutions began to present themselves. Inch by inch, we stripped the film of all the moments that made us cringe with shame. Then we found the footage that sang, dusted it off, and built the film around it.

Toward the end of the edit, Cecilia said something that permanently shifted my perspective: "If someone told me, you can only choose one option—(A) critics love it, we win all the awards; (B) audiences love it, we make all the money; or (C) you and I love it, nobody else really cares—I would always, no question, choose C. All we have control of is making the film we would want to watch." I think about this a lot. It gave me permission to stop trying to imagine how people would perceive what we were making and to hone in on what *I* saw. We made the film we would want to watch. Then, we sent it off to festivals.

I was in Cecilia's kitchen when I saw that I had an email from Kim Yutani, a Sundance programmer (who would soon go on to become the director of programming), asking me to give her a call. We weren't expecting to get a response from them for weeks, so I was convinced it was bad news. "We didn't get in. They're telling us now to put us out of our misery," I said to Cecilia. What I would soon come to learn is that the film industry follows Tinder dating law: rejection comes in the form of ghosting. It's a business that revolves around being liked, so nobody wants to be the guy that said no. Instead they settle for being the guy who said nothing.

When I called Kim her first words were "I have good news." It was truly shocking. I repeated everything she said back to her like a parrot so I could confirm I was hearing her correctly and not hallucinating. Cecilia and I were staring at each other the whole time, eyes wide and eyebrows raised. Our dream had come true. We'd made the film we wanted to make, and that was enough. We had no game, no swagger, no connections, only our taste and belief in each other. The film was put together with spit and good intentions, and somehow it managed to enter a realm of legitimacy I'd been aspiring to since my Vomlet days.

I thought it was the beginning of happiness. I thought that once good fortune shined its light on you, what followed would be a montage of nonstop confidence and winning, but I was wrong. That moment in the kitchen with Cecilia, learning that our film had been accepted into Sundance, wasn't the beginning of happiness, it *was* happiness. I wish I'd savored it longer. Instead, I held on too tight, and the joy wriggled out through my fingers.

On the night of the premiere, just as I was about to step onto the stage to introduce the movie, one of the various Hollywood types that had cannonballed into our lives since our getting accepted into Sundance grabbed me by the arm, looked me dead in the eyes, and said:

TITAN OF INDUSTRY: This is your big moment.
ME: Yup!
TITAN OF INDUSTRY: It's important that you nail it.

ME: I hear you.
TITAN OF INDUSTRY: Make sure you're charming. And funny.
ME: Of course, got it.
TITAN OF INDUSTRY: And self-deprecating. Don't forget to be self-deprecating.
ME: I'm on it!

The last-in/first-out industry players who came on board in the weeks preceding Sundance kept toggling back and forth between annoyance at having to slum it for a tiny film with no stars' first time at the rodeo and self-congratulatory satisfaction at having discovered what they were hoping would become the new face of indie cinema. I accepted all advice with a doglike obedience. Meanwhile, Cecilia was livid. "Do you think Damien Chazelle just got that pep talk?" Chazelle had just opened the festival with *Whiplash*, and no, I couldn't imagine anyone instructing him to keep it humble and self-deprecating, because everyone knows how grotesque confidence is in a girl who looks like she doesn't really deserve to be there.

I got onstage and introduced the film as I had always planned to: "Most girls dream about their wedding day. I dreamt of premiering my first film at Sundance. Welcome to my wedding." It was my greatest moment of triumph. And from then on, everything fell to shit.

As the film played, people kept walking out of the theater, slamming the door loudly behind them. Each door slam felt like a gunshot. And it wasn't a theater as much as it was a hotel lobby, and apparently "the worst venue at the festival," according to all of my handlers. Every twenty minutes, the screen would cut to black for a handful of excruciating seconds. But it wasn't the technical difficulties, the walkouts, or even that wildly demotivating motivational speech that made it a horrible premiere. It was the room. Up until that point, I'd always thought that what set film apart from other media was its consistency: no matter what year it is, what format you're viewing it in, the film remains the same. What I came to learn is that the experience of watching a film is entirely dependent on where you watch it and who you watch it with. In the right room, it feels like a conversation, where everyone's strapped into the same emotional journey and the audience is hungry for more. At the premiere of *Appropriate Behavior*, it felt like a force-feeding. Every joke, emotional beat, and transition fell limp. It felt like the entire audience was just waiting for it to be over, myself included.

About an hour after the screening, I received a text from my brother with a link to the *Hollywood Reporter* review of the film. I'd gone into Sundance with a plan to be the kind of person who, when asked about their thoughts on the critical response to their work, could answer with the only cool reply possible, "I don't read reviews." Not reading reviews is the move, and I knew that. Everyone knows that. But what I didn't know was how impossible it would be to shield myself from the desperate need to prove my worst thoughts wrong. The moment that link appeared on my phone I completely forgot the promise I'd made to myself to be above reading press. I needed solid evidence that the premiere hadn't gone as badly as I'd felt it had, and I figured it must have been a glowing review, otherwise why would my brother have texted it to me?

The review began, "The central character played with deadpan insouciance and minimal dramatic heft by writer-director Desiree Akhavan . . ." It went on to say more things. Meaner things. But the words "minimal dramatic heft" clung to me. "Minimal dramatic heft" rang in my ears while I got dressed the next day. "Minimal dramatic heft" with my morning coffee, as the year marched on from winter into spring. It joined the ranks of all the third-party information I've read or heard about myself that made up my mental picture of the lady in the mirror.

There's a whole rolodex of sound bites from "the Beast" to "minimal dramatic heft" to that time a guy on the subway monologued for eight stops straight about how much I looked like the female incarnation of Spock from *Star Trek*.*

Here's the thing: it's always the wrong choice to read reviews, whether they're positive or negative. They fuck with your head. When someone watches your work and connects to it the same way you have with the films that raised you, it feels ... wild. It's a type of power that's hard to internalize, so you don't. You figure that the person it came from must not have very good taste, or that perhaps they have a personal bias toward the subject matter that tricked them into liking the movie. But if the review is negative and the professional opinion-haver is of the opinion that you suck, the criticism gets carved into your psyche, and now it's yours to carry, whether you agree with it or not. Sometimes, when the takedown is well articulated and valid points are being made, it will make you question your audacity for having taken up space in the first place.

The consensus of that first review and many that came to follow was that I was a less good, wannabe Lena Dunham. "It would probably be horribly reductive to describe Desiree Akhavan's 'Appropriate Behavior' as a lesbian Persian-American 'Girls' knockoff," said *Variety*, "but it wouldn't be entirely inaccurate, either. . . . Its auteur ought to be well worth watching once she starts to find her own voice."

Appropriate Behavior is no masterpiece, but it is 100 percent my voice. To imply otherwise is to say that there's only room for one funny female creator who gets to talk about sex and love in New York. As a viewer, I actively crave *more* funny, fe-

---

*He made me promise to send a passport photo of myself to Steven Spielberg, who would then create a show, *Lady Spock*, that would make me "so rich you could open up your own bank."

male creators who talk about sex and love in New York. Actually, that's a lie. I'd rather the next funny female creator who talks about sex and love be from somewhere different like Montana or Japan, but I digress. My point is that just because the critics thought that everything worth saying had already been said on the subject of being female, shameless, and horny doesn't mean they were right. In fact, I think we barely scratched the surface.

When you release a film, you often get critiqued by the kind of viewer who would never choose to see your film in the first place. You didn't make it to please them, and they know it. It's like fishing for acceptance from your dad's conservative second cousin who doesn't believe in climate change. So yeah, I wish I'd stuck to my original "no reading reviews" plan.

I made Sundance hard for myself. I forgot what an honor it was to be invited to the table and focused on my fear that I'd gotten the worst seat. I kept trying to keep up with the big boys with the big sales and put all my effort into unnecessary bullshit like promotional T-shirts and postcards and parties and an endless quest for the perfect premiere outfit that would scream: I Am a Boss and a Movie Star and the Coolest Bitch You Know.* But despite my fears, it was still a dream come true, and despite the technical glitches and walkouts, the premiere generated an incredible amount of love for such a small movie. It took us eight months to make a modest sale, resulting in a tiny release, but the people who needed the film found it, and with time it built a cult following.

Recently *The New York Times* included it in a roundup of cinematic "gems" to stream, writing that it "caused something of a sensation at the 2014 Sundance Film Festival." It certainly didn't *feel* like a sensation at the time, but it goes to show you

---

* I have yet to find that outfit.

never know the full picture when you're in the thick of it. Nor do you know how the narrative will evolve over the years.

I haven't watched *Appropriate Behavior* since it premiered. I tried a few months after Sundance, when it screened at the Sydney Film Festival, but it was too painful. Suddenly, every flaw, every loose seam, every moment I reached for an emotion

Me and Cecilia on our last day at Sundance

I failed to summon mocked me from the screen. Perhaps you're not meant to watch your films once you've set them free into the world. Alfonso Cuarón nailed it when he said, "For me, my films are not like my children. They are like my ex-wife. They gave me so much; I gave them so much; I loved them so much; we part ways, and it's OK we part ways." I see the work I've made as these beautiful experiments for which I have a lot of tenderness and nostalgia, but not much passion. If you're lucky, by the time your film comes out you'll have moved on to your next obsession, and the cycle will have continued.

First Movies That Will Make You Want to Make a First Movie

- François Truffaut's *The 400 Blows* because it's the original origin story
- P. J. Hogan's *Muriel's Wedding* because it captures the grotesque in fitting in
- Todd Haynes's *Superstar* because it'll inspire you to utilize whatever's at your disposal
- Rob Reiner's *This Is Spinal Tap* because it invented its own genre
- Roman Polanski's *Knife in the Water* because it's the ultimate twenty-four-hour dick-measuring contest
- Marjane Satrapi and Vincent Paronnaud's *Persepolis* because it finds the funny in the devastating (and for its hands-down best use of "Eye of the Tiger" in cinematic history)
- Ousmane Sembène's *Black Girl* because it's like watching a woman scream underwater for fifty-five minutes straight
- Lynne Ramsay's *Ratcatcher* because it sets the bar

- Kevin Smith's *Clerks* because it makes it look like any asshole can do it
- Miranda July's *Me and You and Everyone We Know* (the movie that made me want to make movies) because it made me think I might not be alone in all my loneliness

Boy Crazy

I'm newly single, new to London, and eager to get my clothes off in front of strangers after dropping fifteen pounds due to sadness. I've just turned thirty, and while everyone else is mourning the loss of their twenties, I feel young and free in a way I've never experienced before. I flew in for two weeks of press to promote the UK release of *Appropriate Behavior*, and by the end of it I couldn't bring myself to get on the return flight home, so now I've moved into a tiny half-room off Cecilia's kitchen. It's the kind of room that's big enough to accommodate unfolding the sofa bed or the suitcase, but not both at once.

My girlfriend Star and I have just broken up. For years, she provided the confidence, love, and roof over my head that enabled my first film *and* managed to convince my parents that being gay could look good on paper. She was the first grown-up I'd ever been with: suits to work, doormen in the lobby, and triathlons for funsies. But something wasn't right. We'd been such good kissers, and suddenly our teeth started knocking.

I couldn't imagine New York without her, so I left, but now that I have, I realize it wasn't just New York that I attached to her but every hour of the day. I need to regrow that callused layer of skin that shields you from the quotidian horrors of being out in the world. Without her, I have to make my own coffee and face my own thoughts. I haven't had to face my thoughts alone in a good long time. I passed the role of emotional wet nurse from one girlfriend to the next so quickly, I didn't even realize the position existed until it was vacant. I can turn lust into codependence faster than you can say "lesbian bed death."

It's been a month into life without Star, and I've hit a level of lonely I forgot existed—the kind that leaks out your pores and onto your eyelashes until you're seeing the world through shit-colored glasses: *La Vie en Merde.* I manage the lonely with marathon screenings of the Blockbuster discount bin genre of chick flick, which act as a pacifier that lulls me into numb apathy for the ninety-three-minute run time: *Uptown Girls, 27 Dresses, Kate Hudson Wears a Yellow Dress!*

I need a distraction. New adventures. New faces. I join Tinder.

I haven't been with a man in ages. I'm thirsty for testosterone like the grass might be greener. When it comes to men, I've always felt like the neutered best friend type who enables romantic fun for the beautiful people: the girl holding your purse while you dance in the middle and makes your boyfriend a sandwich after you pass out. But now I'm thirty, and I've finally grown into my face. And I'm technically a movie star (if you ignore the fact that I cast myself in the one movie I'm the star of).

I'm after three things: fun, respect, and good sex. The fact that I expect to find any of that on a dating app is how you know I'm dumb and green. Online dating is real enough to keep me swiping till 4 A.M., but fake enough that I wouldn't be surprised if I found out all my matches were catfishes made by my agoraphobic neighbor who hasn't turned off the radio in four years. It's addictive like Tetris: compulsive swiping that whips you into a false sense of accomplishment. But unlike Tetris, it's got real-life humiliation stakes that aren't visible until you're outside a bar, posing against a brick wall, stealing glances at every passing body while pretending to be in the middle of an urgent text exchange.

My mom's single too, for the first time in her adult life. She tries to give me her copy of that book *The Rules*, the one that teaches women how to be "easy to be with, but hard to get." She says men enjoy the chase and they're hunters by nature. Turns out Mom's a Charlotte. I'm a Samantha without the Pilates ass or the success rate. I can't help myself. Every time I leave the house, I say I'm going out for the chat, the fun, the change of scenery; I tell myself that sex is off the table. Then I get to the bar and find myself ranking the room in order of whose shirt I'd most like to rip off. My standards decline with each hour and each drink, from *Who do I want*, to *Who's up for it*, to *Who's lucid*, until it's last call and I'm scrambling to close the deal with a stringy-haired documentarian who looks like a Picasso interpretation of the scientist from *Short Circuit*. Meanwhile, he's trying to engage the girl to my left, so it's more of a group chat.

I start dating a man twelve years older, only I wouldn't call it "dating": it's more dating *lite*, the type of aimless timesharing that results from meeting someone on your phone because you both need a thing to do that night. He had easy success in his youth, but when we meet, he's straight off a string of failures that have left him sad and bitter.

We have a good first week; nothing beats selectively doling out your Greatest Anecdote Hits with the kind of confidence that comes from having spent twenty minutes applying eyeliner until you got it just right, both of you blissfully unaware of where the other's deficits lie. But then it stops being good. Yet I keep holding on to the memory of this one time we kissed in the park late at night, when the moonlight, city soundscape, and a passing fox all fell into sync like magic.

Our kissing is, without a doubt, the worst kissing I've ever engaged in. His tongue darts in and out of my mouth, staccato and rigid, like a Pap smear. He's stingy with kindness, affection, and covering his portion of the bill, and I know I should delete his number, but I keep engaging like my pussy is Prozac and we're waiting out the initial four- to six-week adjustment period. I just "couldn't help but wonder," is this guy secretly great beneath his midlife crisis? Can I trick him into outgrowing all the traits I hate by staying "chill" long enough? And is this what all straight men are like, or just the ones I let inside me?

One night he takes me to his friend's house party. Everyone in London acts like it's not really a party until the cocaine comes out, and I lose him to the elite few doing lines in the bathroom. It's cool, I'm enjoying the experience of being dropped into a night of all strangers and no context. I can feel eyes on me. I start talking to two guys who trick me into thinking they're Scottish when really they're Italian and really I'm drunk. They're trying to impress me with jokes and funny voices, and it feels so strange because *I've* always been the one with the jokes and the voices doing the heavy lifting to compensate for the shitty visuals. It feels like I'm in a *Freaky Friday* life swap—like somewhere in Kansas there must be a cheerleader being overlooked at a keg party.

They aren't funny, but I laugh. The back of one of their hands keeps grazing against my left breast and I allow it. *Why* do I allow it? I'm not interested in him. I could take a step backward and move my left breast out of the equation, but I don't. I've always been such a vocal critic of the male gaze, but now that I'm the object of it I wanna pitch a tent and set up camp. Luxuriate in it. I'm in the game for the first time, and I want to know what happens next.

But nothing happens next. The dude twelve years my senior takes me home like a consolation prize. Like what he *really* wanted was solitary, introspective time to mourn his youth and the state of capitalism. He goes down on me for maybe four minutes and gets pissy when I don't come. The next day I listen to a podcast where a seventy-seven-year-old Jane Fonda speaks about sex in a way that feels equal parts aspirational and demoralizing:

> I think that when a woman is older, sex is better. Partly be-
> cause she doesn't give a fuzzy rat's ass, you know? She's not
> out there on the marketplace anymore. She knows her body.
> She knows what she wants. She's less afraid to ask for it. If it
> doesn't work out, so what?

Her words haunt me. They expose the shittiness of my sex-capades. It feels like my body is doing an impression of a lady enjoying the sex, while my head's busy censoring all the instincts I know have no place in this room with this man. I don't want to wait until I'm seventy-seven to fuck like Jane Fonda.

I need more practice. I return to Tinder.

I start dating a twenty-five-year-old with mommy issues who looks like (I swear to God) a sexy Mr. Bean. He takes me to a concert at Islington Assembly Hall, and when the minus-cule security guard gives us attitude, he says, "I didn't know they let fourteen-year-old boys do security." And then I spot the soft wrinkles around the guard's eyes and mouth and real-ize she's not a young man but an older dyke, and the moment turns sinister. He's made fun of one of my own, and I go hot with shame. It's my two lifestyles head-butting each other, and

I'm on the wrong side of the fight. I feel like I've betrayed not only this lesbian security guard but every lesbian I've ever known, fucked, or loved.

Inside the concert, I'm mad at him for what he said, but he's already forgotten it, so now I'm also mad at him for that. The man in front of us is holding his date by the waist like he's holding an inflatable guitar. Like he's play-acting at holding a woman. I look around and notice we're surrounded by couples, swaying and holding waists. He glues his head to my shoulder and calls me a cow in a way that he thinks is endearing because he's English, and I find repugnant because I'm not.

I get Tinder–stood up, which feels like a new kind of loss, a nonloss that's surprisingly sharp nevertheless. I stand outside a restaurant on Upper Street from seven to eight on a Friday, trying to decide if going in and having a drink by myself would make the experience more pathetic or less pathetic.

I start dating an aspiring painter who's convinced we're falling in love. He fills my days with a nonstop stream of texts: doodles and pictures and gifs and a collage that paints me as the love child of Julia Roberts and Jim Morrison. One time, in the middle of the night, he demands food and eats an entire pint of yogurt in my bed naked, hunched over and greedy in a way that reminds me so much of Gollum that I feel compelled to photograph it. There's such a fine line between attraction and repulsion.

I don't think we have a future together, but he keeps arguing his case for one: "Fucking hell, Desiree, let's not pretend we don't have feelings for each other!" I'm struck by the confidence with which he assumes my side of the equation. It makes me wonder if he sees something I don't. So I give in. I let myself imagine the possibility of being his, I start replying to the late-night texts, I let him hold my hand in public, and I finally agree to meet his friends. And the day after I do, he ghosts me.

Intellectually, I understand it's no great loss, yet I mourn. I mourn having a dinner to dress for, a body to practice on. He'd said he'd build a staircase for my loft bed so I wouldn't have to use the shaky ladder. I'd invested in silky slips because he liked the feel of them against his skin. Now they mock me from the dresser drawer, still folded with the tags on.

I keep swiping. I accidentally send the guy twelve years my senior a photo of my ass with a big red welt on it that was meant for a sext-crazed experiment I tried one night. It was my one and only X-rated photo, I took it against my better judgment, and of course I sent it to the wrong person.

I go a bit boy crazy, and the more men I date, the more I feel myself becoming a *Cathy* cartoon: I can't trust these guys, can't read their minds, can't relate to their instincts, and *can't* stop waiting for the phone to ring—Aack! Being bisexual is like being fluent in two different languages. Actually, no, I'm full of shit. It's half-speaking both of them—barely enough to get through small talk. Here's what I know. With women it's been intuitive: I like you, you like me; if we're not feeling it we'll respectfully bow out, but if we *are* feeling it, let's merge completely until I don't know where I end and you begin. With men, I can be a closed book: they aren't even looking for the plot beyond the cover. I can't decide which I hate more.

Lesbians can respect a slut. They understand that you can fuck someone and it doesn't mean you've "had" them. Men, not as much. A male friend once told me: "I'm always going to push for sex on the first date, I do it to see if I can, but it tends to depress me and I end up resenting the girl." I'm not sure the men I meet want me to want sex. I think they'd rather trick me into it.

But women can be just as infuriating. Women can have sex on you, not with you. Women can be just as cheap with the bill and stingy with the affection. Perhaps it's not testosterone I crave or estrogen I need, but neither of them?

The end always sneaks up on you when you're dating casually. I can never see the last time I'll ever lay eyes on someone coming, but I always know the moment it's happening. I'm going out with an Australian producer who likes me when he's drinking but not when he's sober. We're at a bar, the stupid kind where the drinks take twenty-five minutes to make and cost as much as your entrée. It's winter, and the heat's turned up so high the windows are all steamed up. He takes off his thick wool sweater to reveal a tissue-thin tank top, which leaves him looking like a wet poodle: all bone, no fluff.

Yeah, it's mildly embarrassing to be sitting with his visible nipples on a Friday night, but I ignore them until the bartender approaches and politely asks that he please put a shirt on. Instead of acquiescing, this guy gets combative. The bartender, while apologetic, doesn't budge. So my date announces, "We're leaving!" And I have no choice, I'm part of the resistance now; we gather our layers and make our way to the exit.

Outside, we're cold and wet with sweat. I know that to make the evening work, all I have to do is join in on his outrage, but I can't muster it. I simply do not give a shit. I don't give a shit about his rage or his sweater or him or any of these guys, nor do they give a shit about me. We're all just passing time, bingeing each other like you would *Love Is Blind:* mindless, compulsive, and a bit disgusted with yourself. It hits me then and there, while I'm holding my layers: neither of us likes the other enough.

I give my date a sympathetic smile as he pulls his sweater on, and say I should get home, I have an early morning. He looks relieved to be rid of me and says he'll call but that the next week is going to be pretty busy. Then he blesses me with an obligatory half-open mouth, quick swipe of the tongue before he turns and walks away.

I watch him jaywalk through the next light and narrowly miss a pile of dog shit. I watch him pass a group of teens flirting, a girl jumping to grab her phone out of the hand of a lanky kid holding it out of reach. I watch until he's out of sight, and then I stand there and watch London. It's massive and glowing and chic and anonymous and brimming with life. I was so afraid to face this place on my own, but now that I think about it that seems absurd. This city is a hub for the lonely. It's where you come to be an island.

So I pull out my phone, delete Tinder, and walk home.

What I Wish
I'd Known at Thirty

- Go ahead and leave the party the moment the impulse hits. If you're not having fun, it's not getting better. Not with more alcohol. Not even with pills.
- Stop putting yourself down. Or, at the very least, stop doing it out loud. It makes you look like you're either pathetic or disingenuous.
- Don't take someone you're dating casually to the places you love most. Chances are the next time you're at your favorite bar you won't be able to escape a hologram of your past self making out furiously with a girl who tried to convince you Kubrick staged the moon landing.
- Nobody innately deserves success. It's a gift, and it can be taken away from you at any moment.
- And if it is, that's okay. Professional success isn't the only measure of a good life.

Homesick

My father's name is Cyrous. The volume of his voice is always turned up to the highest decibel, and he WRITES ALL HIS TEXTS AND EMAILS IN CAPS SO IT FEELS

LIKE YOU'RE BEING YELLED AT WHEN REALLY HE'S
JUST ASKING IF YOU WANT TO GET DINNER ON
WEDNESDAY. He looks like a thicker version of Billy Crys-
tal, sounds like an immigrant, and says things like "I didn't go
to school just to eat my lunch."

He grew up the eldest of four in a large, idyllic home. He's
full of life lessons that come in the form of bite-size adages.
They seem throwaway at first glance, but the longer you live
with them, the more their depth reveals itself to you. When I
came home sobbing after my best friend sucked face with the
boy I'd spent the better part of high school writing (never-
sent) love notes to, he said, "To make a friend you open your
eyes to their good qualities, but to keep a friend you have to
close one eye." When he dropped me off in Times Square so I
could score standing-room tickets to *The Producers* on September 13, 2001, he said, "If you live in fear you die each day, but if
you keep moving forward you only die once." But my favorite
saying of his, the one he says so often it's become a mantra, is
"Fuck 'em if they can't take a joke," which he offers as a cure-all
for whatever ails you, from a broken heart to the wage gap.

My mother's name is Yasmin. She can always guess how
the movie's going to end within the first ten minutes. Her
cheekbones, handwriting, and table settings feel reminiscent of
a different, better era. She looks like a hotter version of Susan
Sarandon, always smells like Salvatore Ferragamo for Women,
takes on the accent of whoever she's speaking to, and says
things like "Be careful, Desi, they put needles with AIDS in
them inside the change slots of public phones."

She was born in Tehran and sent to a British boarding
school when she was six and didn't speak a word of English. A
German woman named Mutti, who ran a boardinghouse in
London, was hired to look after her during school holidays.
For four years, nobody visited her. By the time she was sent

back to Iran, her father had died of cancer, but nobody had the heart to tell her, and he remained "on a business trip" for another year.

My parents' marriage wasn't arranged, it was introduced. I'm still trying to figure out what "introduced" means and where it lands on the spectrum of normal-for-Iran and inhumane-for-the-West. I think it's something along the lines of "It would be cool if you got married, but first go on a few dates and make sure you're into it." When I tell Americans how my mom and dad met, they always ask the exact same question, and I never know how to answer: Were they in love?

I'm confident they were as in love as any introduced Iranian couple could be, but I sometimes wonder if love, marriage, and family mean something completely different in Iran. That's the deal with being the child of immigrants: it strips you of your ability to fully understand both the culture you were born to and the one you were raised in.

The story I've cobbled together is that my father's parents were looking for a wife for him. They reached out to their friends the Rofougarans, who asked *their* friends, the Kashefis, if they knew any good, eligible girls. It turns out they did, and it was decided that the Kashefis would bring said girl to a party at the Rofougarans' home.

When I ask my mother about that first night, she says she wore a flower print chiffon off-the-shoulder dress with strappy heels that she worried made her toes stick out in a weird way. She spent the night hiding her feet with the hem of her skirt. My father arrived hours late and made a big show of how he was only dropping by and would have to leave early. But he didn't leave. Instead, he sat next to her and launched into a nonstop monologue that kept going until two in the morning. Her first impression was that he was a good-looking guy who wouldn't shut up.

When I ask my father about that first night, he says: I don't remember, ask your mother.

The story goes that later that night my father marched into his parents' bedroom and announced that he'd met the woman he was going to marry. He was twenty-six, and she was nineteen. They met in July and married in October of 1978, at the dawn of the Islamic Revolution. At the time, protests against the Shah were pouring into the streets of Tehran, but neither of them took it seriously. Three months after their wedding, the Shah went into exile, and the Imam Ayatollah Khomeini returned from his exile, spearheading the country's violent transition into an Islamic Republic.

Their wedding was a massive, 350-person affair on what turned out to be the last night before martial law and a seven o'clock curfew would be enforced. The next day, the building across the street from their hotel was lit on fire by protesters. In the rush to evacuate, my mother left her wedding shoes behind. Of everything she lost in that period, my mother mourned only two things: those wedding shoes and a journal she'd kept chronicling the revolution that her mother burned out of fear it would be found by the authorities and seen as anti-Islamic propaganda. Sometimes I have a hard time believing these are the stories that make up my parents' past, and not a plot lifted off a telenovela.

There aren't many pictures from my parents' lives in Iran, except for a thin blue leather-bound album of wedding photos. My mother's dress is pure '70s glamour: scooped neck, huge bell sleeves, and layers upon layers of lace that grew into a massive A-line skirt with about five feet of train. My father wore two suits with the exact same slim-fit, double-breasted, bell-bottom cut, white for the ceremony and black for the reception. They're photos not just of a different time but of a different universe. The album is my only evidence of a prerevolutionary Iran that no longer exists: colorful, glamorous, hedonistic, and slightly sepia hued.

This is my mother on her wedding day, dancing the way Persians dance: like her arms are serpents, like it's a call-and-response between her neck and her shoulders.

This was the ceremony. The floating head above them is my grandmother, Mahin, who's grinding two large cones of sugar wrapped in lace above their heads, to symbolize sprinkling sweetness onto their marriage.

This is Googoosh, the biggest Iranian pop star of all time, singing at the reception. It was most likely her final performance before women were banned from singing publicly.

These are the guests, waiting for the dessert plates to be cleared.

These are my parents. She has a migraine and is trying to hide it, while he's deeply uncomfortable being the center of attention.

Within twenty-four hours of these pictures being taken, life as they knew it was over. A week after the wedding, the Shah went on television and gave a speech: "I've heard the voice of your revolution." And my father thought, "Shit. He's giving up." Months later, in January of 1979, the Shah and his family left Iran for good, and from that moment on there was no law. Every neighborhood assembled a volunteer watch group to patrol the streets. Anyone they knew who had ties to the Shah and the previous regime either fled the country or went missing. Secular friends suddenly grew beards and started masquerading as devout. A group of militarized college students took control of the US Embassy, holding fifty-two US diplomats and citizens hostage. At night, vendors sold grilled corn and soda outside the embassy, and hundreds of people would show up and walk around like it was a carnival. There was even a small exhibit displaying shredded US government documents that had been reassembled during the siege.

We never talked about any of it. Growing up, there was absolutely no mention of my parents' lives during the revolution. Over the years, I've piecemealed together memories I've pried out of various family members. They play like a slideshow in my head:

- Empty aisles at the supermarket
- A mad sprint home to burn contraband before the authorities get there
- Arriving at a friend's house for dinner to find them missing and their house ransacked
- Candlelit shadow puppets prancing from wall to wall during nightly blackouts
- Falling asleep each night to a chorus of thousands chanting DEATH TO AMERICA

- My pregnant mother getting sucked into a riot on her way home from the store, and the miscarriage that followed

My brother, Ardavan, was born a year later in 1980. He was two months premature and looked like a bird, all bone and folded skin—so tiny his little mouth couldn't latch on to breastfeed, so they fed him with an eye dropper. The hospital was overrun and undersupplied. They ran out of thread to stitch my mother back up, so my father had to go from pharmacy to pharmacy, searching all over Tehran to find some. Or at least that was what I was told. When I asked my father to tell me the story again so I could get the details right, he said, "That never happened. It was my friend Amir-Ali who had to get thread for his wife. They had everything at the hospital when Ardavan was born."

Here's the thing: you can't take anything your Iranian parent tells you at face value. My mother says there was no thread, my father says there was, and that's all the information I get. They're like this with everything. The truth shape-shifts. They'll add a dash of deception (rationalizing that some things you're better off not knowing), a healthy dose of dramatic liberty (I like to think of it as an innate sense of showmanship and commitment to really "land" the story), and, finally, a pinch of genuine confusion over what's real and what's the story they told themselves in order to survive (the truth probably lies somewhere between the two). She sees red where he sees blue, and each time I ask them about the past I get conflicting answers. The longer they were married, the further their truths drifted away from each other.

Here are the facts: they left Iran in May of 1980, forty days after Ardavan was born. The airports were chaos at that time, so they arrived for their flight twenty-four hours early and spent each of those hours slowly inching their way through the maze of bodies desperate to flee. My exhausted father fell asleep the moment the plane took off, leaving my mother to deal with their screaming newborn. By the time he opened his eyes and reached out to relieve her of the baby, the plane had already landed in Paris. This is the only story where both of their accounts align.

In Paris, they squeezed into a small apartment with my dad's family. When they met up with friends, they'd say, "Next month, I'll see you in Iran!" But four months after they left, Iraq launched a full-scale invasion into Iran, beginning a war that lasted almost eight years. By the time I was born in 1984, my parents had moved to the States. I was born in New York Hospital. Both my height and weight were in the ninetieth percentile, and I latched immediately. Any hopes of returning home were long dead, or they wouldn't have given me a Western name. They'd originally wanted to call me Assieh but decided having a name that shortened to "ass" in English might not be the best thing to saddle a kid with (and I remain grateful for that consideration). Ardavan became "Eddie," I became "Desi," and we became an American family.

In Iran, my father ran a successful business importing steel. In the States, he hustled, embarking on one enterprise after another, reinventing himself with each one, from the importing of jewelry and handbags to textile manufacturing, then real estate. My mother worked in retail and as a gemologist in a series of miserable jobs. My parents worked long hours, commuted four hours a day, and used every last cent they'd brought over from Iran to pay for my brother and me to attend one of the most prestigious private schools in the country.

As latchkey kids with a glut of unsupervised after-school time to burn, Ardavan and I spent our formative years on the couch, glued to the television. We learned what it was to be

American through daily marathon sessions of *Diff'rent Strokes*, *The Brady Bunch*, *Liquid Television*, *Beavis and Butt-Head*, *Daria*, *Who's the Boss*, *MADtv*, *Happy Days*, *The Cosby Show*, *The State*, *The Critic*, *The Simpsons*, *The Tracey Ullman Show*, *The Beverly Hillbillies*, *A Different World*, *Full House*, *Fresh Prince*, *Saved by the Bell*, *Family Matters*, *In Living Color*, *Tales from the Crypt*, and *The Kids in the Hall* (which is Canadian but still had an impact). Everything I know about sex, sports, prom, Christmas, dogs, cheerleading, a well-balanced meal, and insurance I learned from a television (I may not know that much about sports or insurance). My brother had permanent control over the remote except for one day a year, when he'd throw it at me around midnight and say, "Happy Birthday. You have twenty-four hours."

Ardavan is a movie buff in the purest sense of the term. Sometimes he'll flip through channels, and we'll make a game of who can name what's playing before he flips to the next. Besides his work, I don't think there's a single thing he loves more than watching and forming an opinion on what he's watching. Ninety percent of our conversations revolve around those opinions. He's the reason I make movies—I do it to impress him. He's the funniest person I know, and I formed my sense of humor watching him watch the screen. For the longest time it was just the two of us parked silently in front of a television. We had all the fictional friends we could want and absolutely zero real-world party invitations, being social outcasts whose mother insisted on dressing us well into our teens. Neither one of us knew how to assimilate.

Being the child of immigrants is like being born a widow: the loss is baked into you. You're intrinsically homesick for a place that you've never known and that no longer exists the way your family remembers it. Our home was a testament to an Iran locked in time: Qajar paintings of unibrowed women playing the sitar, handwoven carpets in deep jewel tones, and replicas of stone carved busts from Persepolis littered throughout the house. The music we played was Persian, dated, and featured way too much electric keyboard. We didn't go tailgating, we went to *mehmoonies:* parties where there were no fewer than fifty guests, ranging in age from zero to one hundred. Dinner was never served before eleven, and you'd dance so hard you left with pit stains.

The Farsi I was taught to speak is antiquated and formal, "May your hands not hurt" instead of "Thanks." It felt like a secret language our parents had made up so we could talk shit about strangers in elevators. I kept half-expecting them to start cracking up and admit we were Hispanic and that the whole Iran thing was a joke that had gone too far.

Being Iranian in the diaspora means gossip is our love language; hours are spent breaking down the details of one another's lives, not because we're assholes, but because we "care." Because we're family. Even when we're technically not, we become your "aunties" or "cousins," and therefore *your* business is *our* business. But mostly because it's so damn fun, and we're honest-to-god storytellers, each and every one of us, exaggerating just shy of making up half the shit we repeat through the grapevine.

It's bringing the drama and taking everything way too seriously and way personally. While my father was planning my brother's wedding, I heard him scream, "THEY WANT KABOB, WE WANT FILET. THIS IS WAR, AND I DO *NOT* INTEND TO LOSE."

It's adhering to a complete reversal of the Western hierarchy, with the elderly at the top of the respect ladder and children at the very bottom. When I first visited Iran, I watched a children's game show where the host openly mocked the ten-year-old contestants: "Wrong answer again, Kamyar! Earlier in the program you said you wanted to be a doctor when you grow up, but tell me, how is that gonna happen when you're so dumb you can't even answer a simple game show question?"

It's learning American colloquialisms just a *little* bit wrong, like how I thought it was "You can't find money in a bush" or "I beg the difference!" In fact, up until college I pronounced it pome*ne*granate, which is particularly tragic since pomegranates play such a large role in Persian cuisine.

It's being obsessed with status. It's suffocating your ugliest memories and pretending they never happened. It's *tarof*, that social obligation to constantly offer up everything you've got, whether or not you want to give it, and it's built into my bones. All of this Persian shit is.

Because my fate was redirected before I was born, I've always felt like I was stuck in an art house *Sliding Doors* remake. During the Revolution, a path divided in the road between life as an Iranian in Iran and the exact opposite of that life in America. I grew up haunted by the question: Who would I have been if my family hadn't left? Would I speak with my hands more? Would I dress differently? Smell different? Have more friends, no friends? Would I be rich? Would I be happy? Because in this country I felt like I made no sense.

Does the alternate, hijabi Desiree make sense in Iran? Would she be queer, and capable of juggling the double life required for that kind of underground existence in a place where being gay is punishable by death, or would she have cut off that part of herself for the sake of safety? Most important, would she be brave enough to put her life on the line to stand up to an oppressive regime? Recently, one of my aunts said she wasn't sure if she had the right to call herself an Iranian woman, since the title now carries a fearlessness and courage none of us outside the country could ever imagine taking on.

In my twenties, at the behest of a friend, I went to an astrology shop in London to get my chart read. This was back in the dark ages before there were eight different star-based social networking apps to choose from. The man who ran the shop took my birth date, time, and location, plugged them into his ancient desktop, and printed out a little booklet that I immediately lost and forgot about forever, but what I do remember is what the man said right after he examined my chart: "You will never have a home. You'll travel and search and have adventures, and you'll never find your home." He went on to explain what sign in what house confirmed this fate, but I couldn't hear because "You will never have a home" was echoing too loudly in my head. At that age, his words felt like a gift. Up until that point in my life, "home" was synonymous with "prison," and I was eager to run as far from it as I could. Now that my parents have divorced and that home's been destroyed, I wonder if it wasn't a curse.

Like the boy who cried wolf, my parents cried divorce, over and over, for as long as I can remember. I'm so gullible I bought it every time. I'd mourn the loss and prepare myself for a new life, only to find them reunited and suffering from memory loss: "Of course we're not getting divorced. Why the long face? You act like you want us to break up." My dad said it was a percentage game: "If you're happy 60 percent of the time and unhappy 40 percent, the odds are still in your favor." I remember hearing that and thinking, *You're playing real fast and loose with those percentages, buddy.*

My parents fought exclusively in Farsi. For everyday talk, they'd slip in and out, but when they were going for the jugular, it was Farsi all the way. And they fought a lot, in epic, violent, mind-melting sessions.

I can't gauge the severity of curse words in Farsi. I understand the literal translations, but I never know how much punch each one packs, because you can't really translate Farsi into English in a linear, word-for-word way. Farsi is like poetry: it dances around its point, dips a toe in, then moonwalks into a metaphor. The consonants lend themselves to a certain cadence that drips with whatever emotion you inject into it. When delivered with the right amount of disdain, it can hit the ear viscerally. Scream it and the whole house shakes. Whisper it and it's like you're spraying venom. I heard "SNAKE POISON!" screamed so loud and so often that I knew it was hateful, but to this day I'm not quite sure how bad of a bad word it is. "Snake poison" may be the worst thing you could say to a person, or it could be as benign as "darn it."

But divorce was never an option. It simply wasn't done. The appearance of perfection was always the top priority for the insular group of Iranian families we lived among. My mother's high school yearbook quote read, "One should live life like a duck. Calm and serene on the surface but paddling like hell underneath." That quote came to represent everything I hated about growing up in that home. We were always paddling like hell, with big false smiles plastered onto our faces.

When I came out of the closet, it was my parents who faced the gossip, shame, and pity of every Persian in the tristate area. Meanwhile, I centered my gayness on-screen and won prizes for it. I didn't just survive despite my scandal—my scandal became my superpower. Sometimes I wonder if watching me get rewarded for being "bad" was what gave my parents permission to finally get divorced after surviving a revolution, three continents, and thirty-eight years of marriage.

My mother's changed since the divorce. Now she sings to herself without realizing it, takes long walks in Central Park, and talks like a quote-of-the-day calendar, sending me texts like "Good morning, my beautiful daughter, make it a magical day! You are strong and resilient and you can do anything you put your heart and soul into! ♥⚱♥⚱♥☺👏👏👏👏👏👏☀ 👏 👏⚱👏👏◎♥"

"I never realized how good pasta tastes!" she said recently between mouthfuls of linguini one year into their separation. "Lately I'm hungry all the time." She said it with this big, sweet grin on her face, and I felt my whole body stiffen as I struggled to recognize the woman who raised me. I realized I'd never seen her relish a meal in my life. She must have been so tense for so long.

My father's different too, lighter. He's always been pathologically friendly, but now that he's free to say or do whatever he wants he talks like a joke-of-the-day calendar: "Desi, did you know I run ten miles every single morning? . . . Right, before I wake up!" When a waiter asks if he enjoyed his meal, I think it would be physically painful for him not to reply, "Hated it, didn't even touch it!" while presenting a clean plate.

I'm happy they're happy. I'm glad they've been freed. But sometimes I miss my family. Not the version we are now, broken into small, bite-size pieces with our individual, one-on-one dinners and meetups, but the way we used to be: an enmeshed island of four, trapped and miserable in the house we shared at the end of a dead-end road. I'd dreamed of our emancipation for years. I'd wished all my wishes, from birthday candles to rogue eyelashes, for peace and calm and autonomy. But now that I have them, I'm lost.

I miss Farsi. I rarely hear it these days, and when I do it's out of the mouths of strangers on the street. It's both weirdly intimate and deeply alienating to hear the secret language you've spoken only with your parents and grandparents and aunties and uncles outside the context of your living room. It makes the hairs on my arms stand up.

I miss the tiny cardamom chickpea cookies that crumble on your tongue and taste like chalk to my American palate. I miss the mismatched bedsheets that lay draped over every piece of furniture and only came off when there was company. I miss the massive gold samovar that took up 80 percent of the kitchen counter. I miss saffron-flavored sugar sticks in hot water to cure a stomachache. I miss eating celery stew to a soundtrack of *Jeopardy!* followed by *Wheel of Fortune* and then a full hour of *The Simpsons* and absolutely zero conversation. I miss the smell of all the onion frying it took to make that celery stew and how it lived in your hair and your clothes for days. I miss the sound of *esfand* (our version of sage, burned to cleanse you and your house of evil eyes) sizzling on the kitchen stove. I miss *mehmoonies* and *tarof* and walking under the Koran and kissing it at the front door before leaving for a flight and how it made you feel like you were cloaked in an invisible shield of armor, even though I wasn't even sure I believed in God. I miss how we belonged to one another, even though I hated it. Even though I was the first to bail.

I miss my family and they miss Iran, though they'll never admit it, because USA #1 is the mantra of the new American. Where is our home? The astrologist was right; I keep searching for it. We're so much better off now, but here we're tetherless. The permanently homesick; neither Iranian nor American, but a Frankenstein of Middle Eastern heart and values and intimacy sewn into Western ambition and individualism, and we are the only ones of our kind. The longer we're here, the further we grow apart. Soon we'll become extinct.

Letter to a Young Filmmaker

WHAT THEY DON'T TELL YOU is that making bad art is the path every single person takes to making the good stuff.

That you might not make a living at this (at least not for a while).

That one of the biggest hacks to becoming a director is having the audacity to go ahead and call yourself one before anyone else does.

That it really isn't who you know but what you make. Even when it seems like the well connected are leapfrogging ahead at lightning speed.

That every single movie you love was complete shit at one point.

That a lot of being a working artist is keeping your cool when things go haywire.

That finding your voice is something you'll have to do over and over again.

That art won't heal your wounds. It can empower you. It'll

give you a new perspective on the story you told yourself, and sometimes it'll bring you joy you didn't even know existed. But it won't fix the pain that drove you to make it in the first place.

That the fear never goes away.

That there isn't an award that's going to convince you to stop hating yourself.

That art is about connection, not status, and if you confuse one for the other, you're fucked.

That it's easy to delude yourself into thinking you deserve all the credit. You don't, and it's your job to dole it out to the right parties.

That you'll inevitably face a fork in the road where you'll have to choose between chasing your taste and chasing a paycheck.

That sometimes you need to put your pen down, go to the cinema, and pay to sit in a room full of strangers and feel some feelings so you can remember that it's not about you, it's about a higher calling: it's about movies.

That the last thing you need is advice. You'll be fine.

Like Storm from
X-Men

I'm newly single, newly moved into a barely habitable warehouse with a handful of strangers and no windows, and I need a look. A look that explains my whole deal instantly. And by "explains my whole deal," I mean sells me as the coolest, hottest woman in a ten-mile radius. Once that clicks into place, it'll be like none of this ever happened.

My ex used to model. Not as her main source of income, but here and there, and once to pay her way while backpacking through Asia; the effortless cash-grab of a woman blessed with a face and body without bad angles. A mutual friend put us in touch when I needed a place to crash in her city, and when she opened the door, her face, height, and accent turned me speechless and stupid. She was hands down the most attractive human I'd ever encountered, a perfect hybrid of all the best qualities either gender has to offer: six feet tall with Dax-coated hair and a James Dean uniform of white T-shirts and dark indigo jeans. Her face was equal parts pretty and handsome, like a *Romeo and Juliet*–era Leonardo DiCaprio. It felt surreal, the way she materialized in front of me, like she was yanked off of a wet-dream mood board. I took one look at her and broke into a giant, goofy grin that took up half my face and made it impossible to keep a single card to my chest.

Twenty-four hours later we were kissing, and I was in love: head over heels, Cupid bow-and-arrow style, like in the cartoons. The kind of love that makes no sense, has no logic, and is a fact before it's a question. It was an out-of-body experience. Wait, no, it was an in-body, out-of-brain experience. My brain floated up to the ceiling, looked down at us, and laughed at the absurdity of the situation. We'd just met, and she had all of me.

A strong, silent type whose ears don't perk at the sound of gossip, she loved *Alien* above all movies and would have chosen waterboarding over "processing." She owned her apartment and never met a DIY challenge she couldn't master. She hadn't exercised a day in her life, but her body looked like it was chiseled by Romans, which was probably God's way of rewarding her for being the type of person who gives up her bedroom and insists on sleeping on a mattress in the kitchen when a guest she's never met comes to stay for the weekend (which is exactly what she insisted on doing with me that first night).

We spent our days writing on opposite sides of the same room. Around three or four in the afternoon, I'd spiral into a manic state over my inability to make any progress with work and march through the nonstop rain to buy groceries and cook an elaborate three-course meal for two that I'd inevitably eat 80 percent of myself.

Nine months in, the intensity of our incompatibility was as undeniable as that first kiss:

I love you, but we can't watch films with subtitles.
I love you, but you gave me four instructional books on
    the female orgasm for my birthday.

I love you, but you don't get the pain that haunts me.

I love you *because* you don't get the pain that haunts me?

I love you, but when you try to help, you take me further away from my intention.

I love you, but the things I don't love I have no poker face for.

We weren't a good match. I knew it in Berlin, when I opened the door of my bathroom stall just as she stumbled out of hers with three friends, noses caked in four different kinds of speed, and I was repelled—not by the drugs, but by the fact that she was wasting them on such a lame Berlinale party, where the music sucked and old dudes kept grabbing her because they thought she was a twink.

I knew it when we saw *Dheepan* and I cried through the last act and the credits and into our first beer at the pub across the street like a fucking maniac, and she just stared at me from across the table. She couldn't even touch me. I don't blame her—I was, as I said, crying like a fucking maniac. I didn't know how to control myself, and I could see her repulsion grow with every snotty sniffle.

We went on "a break."

I'm cool with it! It's two weeks in and I'm happy. Relieved. It was mutual. We both wanted it. You know what else I want? I would like to be hot. Right now I feel flat and dull and like all the joy's been sucked out of me through my heart. But if I *looked* better, I'd *feel* better, right? So I bleach my hair white, convinced it'll make me look like Storm from *X-Men*.

I bleach my hair thinking it'll be my permanent statement piece, edgy and wild. I bleach my hair because my ex's beauty brings me to my knees, and I'm hoping new hair will push me into the kind of high-impact, hot person status she inhabits. I bleach my hair because an old therapist once told me I'd have more confidence if only I got a makeover. I bleach my hair because I'd like to feel beautiful, the way I did when she first looked at me, but not much since. I bleach my hair hoping that she'll take one look at me and realize she's got it all wrong. I bleach my hair because the crazy keeps convincing me that every single one of my problems can be traced back to the way I look.

From now on, I'll be the director with the white hair! Like John Waters and his tiny mustache or Agnes Varda and that ombre bowl cut. It will be my signature. It's starting to feel like I can't afford NOT to bleach my hair. *This* will be the defining moment. From now on, life will be divided into before and after I found my look.

"Did you do it yourself?" people ask me.

That is how I know I did not find my look.

No, I didn't do it myself. I spent more money on this stupid dye job than I did on rent. Not only did I pay a professional to do this to me over the course of eight hours, I went in a week earlier for a consultation. I did the fucking scratch test for allergies. I made a Pinterest board of hair inspiration and sent it to her via text. This was not an impulsive decision. For months, every time I passed a mirror, I saw a better version of myself staring back with white-blond hair. It haunted me, calling out, *What are you afraid of? Why are you holding back?* It felt like my gut was telling me something.

My gut was wrong. You hear stories about people's instincts leading them away from things like pyramid schemes, questionable leftovers, and plane crashes. My gut led me right into the most overplayed breakup cliché of all time: I fucked with my hair, hoping it would reinvent me, and now I look like Glenn Close in *Fatal Attraction*.

The bleach dulls my normally curly hair into what looks like a broom growing out of my scalp: stiff, yellow, and dry. It feels like a cheap wig. Even if it weren't so damaged, the color doesn't suit my skin tone. How did I forget the fact that I'm Middle Eastern, and olive skin looks terrible against a curtain of blond? There's a reason all the inspiration pictures on my Pinterest board were of East Asian models and St. Vincent. *Of course* they look good with this stupid white hair; they're incredibly pale and professionally good looking. It's their *job* to make stupid things look hot and aspirational to trick you into hemorrhaging cash.

The hair becomes my obsession as I hop from salon to salon, desperate to find the look that'll suit me. I learn that when it comes to coloring your hair, it always takes about two hours longer than they say it will, and the color turns four shades more yellow as soon as you wash it. I spend a good chunk of my time marinating in chairs, cradling stacks of magazines. Like a patient in a hospital, I come alive when the colorist visits my station, frantically trying to frisk her for knowledge.

I cannot let the hair defeat me. If I could just get the right person to give me the right advice, and direct me toward the right products, I could get the good hair, which will bring the beauty, which will bring the confidence, which will bring her back.

Because I miss her. Desperately. I miss how each week I'd pick up a new Scottish-ism/her-ism to add to my lexicon—like *naff*, which is the perfect combination of cheesy and tacky, or *good chat*, which is what she calls you if she thinks you're fun to hang out with. She yelled, "COWBOYS!" when she discovered that the previous owners of her flat had painted the walls without bothering to take down the shelves or electrical outlet covers, leaving behind little rectangles of the previous wall paint in their wake. She taught me that if an American says "space ghetto" it sounds exactly like "Spice Girl" with a Scottish accent, and when I'd do it, we'd laugh until our sides ached, even though it wasn't really *that* funny. When there were guests, nobody went home until every last drop of whiskey in the apartment had been consumed. She was a good host; more than that, she was a genuinely *good* person.

Our Christmas together was my happiest. I'd never seen traditions and games and stuffed stockings and such crispy roast potatoes all squeezed into one pleasant holiday with absolutely no aggression, passive or outright. I made her family pomegranate stew and *tahdig* and a saffron rice pudding that none of us liked but everyone ate out of politeness.

A month into the breakup and two weeks into the bleached hair, I realize I've made a huge mistake, so I tell her I'd like to stop the "break," to which she responds, "No thank you." And that's it. There's nothing I can say to convince her, now that the love I took so easily, greedily, all-you-can-eat-buffet-style is gone.

It feels like the hair is revealing the truth of me: the grasping at cool and getting it four shades too yellow. Sometimes, when the bad luck starts to snowball, I find myself believing in the presence of a higher power. Not God, but more like . . . Satan? A force for banal evil. *You did this to yourself,* I think when I look into the mirror. *You pushed away the one you love and it made you feel ugly, so you made yourself even uglier trying to fix it. You wasted a fortune for the privilege.*

I dye the hair gray, then yellow, then lilac, then purple, then fuchsia. I tell myself how much stronger our relationship will be on the other side of the "break." I tone the hair, condition the hair, cut the hair, oil the hair. I tell myself that this is a test, and it's shown me she's the love of my life. Earning her back will become my biggest triumph. I'm going to tell our kids about this one day. I'm going to tell them how I fucked up and took her for granted, and how it was the best hard lesson of my life.

But six months pass, and she never calls. I keep wishing I could rewind time back to when she liked me. I'd do it all differently: I'd be a patient nurse, I'd let her choose the movies, I wouldn't be so loud and emotional and hard to please.

I call and melt at the sound of her voice. She sounds inconvenienced by mine. I selectively report the highlights of my life with a level of cheery enthusiasm that makes me feel like the host of a dating show. I say I miss her. She doesn't reply.

I say, "You sound like you want nothing to do with me."

And she says, "That's a harsh way to put it, but . . . yeah."

And I realize this will be the last time we speak.

Yes, we don't work, but I was hoping I could transform into the kind of person who *could* work, starting with the "look." But now all I see in the mirror is a stranger. A stranger with pubes for hair.

She knows every shade of me: lazy and half-asleep first thing in the morning, goofy and hyper post shower, abruptly moody for absolutely no reason at around four in the afternoon. She knows how I procrastinate and snack and floss and cry and come. She knows me, and she doesn't want to know anymore.

Slowly, the bleached hair grows out as new hair grows in. "Virgin hair" is what they call it. I harden and harden until the part of me that craves her scabs over. Days pass where I don't think of her at all. And I begin to hope for something better. Better than even that one Christmas with the stockings. I begin to hope for someone who'll want to know *why* I cried so hard during *Dheepan*.

Eventually, she'll just be the girl I bleached my hair for.

The Love of My Life

Cecilia was alone when she found out she was pregnant. She felt like a bomb had gone off. She stared at herself in the mirror and wondered if she'd ever be the same. It was spring. I lived two stops away from her on the overground. Our work was finally hitting its stride—we were in the middle of editing our second film, *The Miseducation of Cameron Post*, and writing our first TV series, *The Bisexual*, which was scheduled to film that winter. She and her husband had just started trying. She had thought it would be like buying a house, where the process of searching and persisting through the various false starts stretches the journey out for years. She thought she'd have time to finish the movie, shoot the show, and wrap her brain around the idea of becoming a mother before she'd have to face the reality of it, but then she went and got pregnant on the first try.

She was terrified to tell me, so she didn't. She knew my reaction would be informed by what the pregnancy would mean for our work. Sure, I'd pretend to be happy for her, but she'd see right through me—that's what years of codependence affords you: complete, unconsensual honesty. How could she watch me pretend to be happy for her when she wasn't even sure if she was happy for herself?

First she told her husband. A few weeks after that she flew to Milan and told her family. There wasn't much fanfare: her mom lit a cigarette, her dad offered her a Limoncello, and her sister started crying. Between sobs she muttered, *"Tra i coglioni"* (which roughly translates to "It'll be between our balls forever").

She broke the news to me at Lardo, our favorite Italian place, equidistant to both our homes. As soon as I registered the words passing her lips, I jumped up to hug her and ended up knocking over both our waters. Then I announced to the entire restaurant, "Sorry! My best friend's having a baby AND I AM VERY HAPPY ABOUT IT!" Tears sprang to my eyes— tears of joy, I told her. *You're feeling emotional because you're happy for your friend!* I told myself, but I was heartbroken. I knew everything was about to change, and I was desperate for it not to. Our lives were woven together. Our days were shaped by a steady stream of communication. From the minute I woke up to the moment my eyes closed at night, we were talking, strategizing, and building: writing scripts, shaping the edit, watching films, and mining our personal lives for characters and stories. It felt as if we'd single-handedly turned hang time with your best friend into a career.

I'd call her "the love of my life," and it didn't matter that I wasn't the love of hers and that she had a husband, because we shared the work, and for me the work was more sacred than sex. Most of our friends were also collaborators. In fact, we'd just spent a few weeks in New York, editing *The Miseducation of Cameron Post* while camping out in our editor Sara's basement and having the time of our lives. It felt like a nonstop sleepover, the kind I never really had as a kid on account of being such a social pariah.

I'd known she was eventually going to have children. I'd hoped that I would too. I just wasn't ready for her to start so soon. We were thirty-three, but I felt like we were in a very special episode of *Teen Mom*. None of our friends had kids. We were all still focused on proving ourselves. There was a lot that intimidated me about motherhood. I might have been in my thirties, but I was just beginning to come into my own and break free from my family, which had only been possible because of Cecilia. She gave me the love and security, the calm chill of a grandparent, and the constant piss-taking of a sibling. Best of all, our friendship was fruitful! We *made* things together and got *better* at making things each year. I could have lived my whole life two stops away from her flat in Cannonbury, picking up coffees and cardamom buns on the way over, spending my days writing and scheming and dreaming up bigger and better stories to tell.

It wasn't just my career, it was *ours*. "I struggled to believe in myself, but I knew I could believe in Desiree" is what she'd say in interviews. We were a joint package—when someone complimented the work, it was *us* they were complimenting. When I was offered a project to consider, I'd send it straight to her so we could discuss whether *we* wanted it or not. We co-created and shared what it was to be "Desiree Akhavan." But the moment she started building a family, I knew I was back on my own.

At first, we encouraged each other into a mutual delusion that having a child wouldn't change anything. "I'll still be the same person!" she promised, committing to board a ten-hour flight to Utah weeks after giving birth for the Sundance premiere of *The Miseducation of Cameron Post*. I decided we'd be the first television production to provide on-set childcare, not really understanding the fact that we were working with a tiny British comedy budget and two location moves a day. She decided she'd come to work with the baby strapped to her chest and one day show them pictures of their first weeks on earth, straight from womb to set. Neither of us had any idea of what we were getting into—with the baby or the show. We thought we could have it all: the boundaryless friendship, the blind ambition, *and* the white picket fence!

Nobody ever wants to be the person who said no. It's a British thing *and* a Hollywood thing, and it wasn't until her due date was looming that someone gently informed us that it *might* not be the best idea to bring a newborn to set, since the fog machine alone would fuck up their lungs, and it became increasingly clear that our plans of sidestepping the limitations of motherhood might be in vain.

The night Cecilia went into the hospital to give birth was when I began to feel the divide between us form. It felt like she was advancing into the highest realm of womanhood—one that I had absolutely no frame of reference for. I resented that I got so little information from her during the week she was in the hospital. I had no way of even picturing it. All I knew was that at one point the nurses started referring to her and her sister as "the lesbians." As in, "The lesbians are complaining again . . ." And I resented that too, because if *anyone* should have the privilege of a hilarious anecdote of mistaken lesbianism, shouldn't it have been me? Hadn't I earned the right? I resented the joke, but more than anything I resented that from that moment on I had to carry the weight of the show and the scripts without her. And I knew I couldn't admit it to anyone because a human life trumps petty resentment, and any nonsociopath knows that the official party line is "What a blessing!" Who wants to be the bitter single workaholic who thinks their needs trump the miracle of life? But I was mad. It felt like we had all the time in the world to have children but such a brief window to chase the opportunities in front of us. Why did she have to choose *this* moment?

The truth that was too embarrassing to say out loud was that I'd never have *considered* making a decision without her, from what outfit to wear to what partner to choose, while she hadn't taken me into account when making the biggest decision of her life. And how could she have? I wasn't her family, even though she'd become mine.

A few weeks after she gave birth, *The Miseducation of Cameron Post* won the grand jury prize at Sundance. The world premiere was hands down the most perfect moment of my professional life. The sold-out Eccles Theater audience of 2,468 people were in the palm of my hand through the entire film. Every beat hit: the funny, the dark, the heart, the lust—I could actually *feel* the whole room feel every last intention. I'd never experienced anything like it, nor have I since, and it should have been ours to share, but she missed it.

She held on to the dream of attending the premiere for as long as possible. She'd written emails from the hospital that said, "See you in Park City!" But after giving birth, she was told that the altitude could be a problem for a newborn. Even if it wasn't, she wasn't sure she could hack it herself. Her body had been torn apart in ways she couldn't have anticipated. Cecilia was the reason the film existed: she'd pushed us forward every time I had a crisis of faith, she'd shaped every scene, every character, every crew member, every rough cut, and sharing it felt empty without her.

A few weeks after the premiere, I began filming *The Bisexual*, and everything that could have gone wrong went wrong. Each second of that shoot felt like a waking nightmare, and as the shitstorm grew worse and worse, Cecilia kept visiting set. It drove me insane. Physically she was there, but mentally she'd completely checked out. One night I found myself butt naked, writhing on the ground as we shot a sex scene, and all I could think was *This is wrong. Everything about this shot and this whole scene is wrong.* I called cut and excused myself. I pulled Cecilia aside and she agreed, "Yeah, it's not right . . ." and then there was silence. She couldn't even brainstorm or ask questions—nothing. She just stared back at me with big blank eyes. Where was the girl who'd knocked down the door to the bathroom when we shot the practically threesome scene in *Appropriate Behavior*? I'd grown so dependent on our ability to share a mind and a shorthand that I had no idea how to work without her.

I grew angrier and meaner by the hour. Her face was a re-minder of everything I'd lost, and I would have rather not seen her at all than see her sporadically and silent. I felt as if she was coming to set to prove to herself that she could "have it all" and doing it at my expense. Meanwhile, Cecilia felt as if her career was happening without her. She was sacrificing a job she'd been preparing for her whole adult life to jump head-first into the brand-new job of motherhood, where she had absolutely no experience and the stakes were life-and-death. But I refused to see it from her perspective. Every story I'd ever heard about motherhood up until that point was about how everyone falls punch-drunk in love with their baby from the first moment they're placed onto their chest. It seemed deeply unfair that she got to fall in love while I was drowning in the work we'd built together. I'd never felt more alone in my life.

Meanwhile, Cecilia was living her own nightmare. Having a child had unleashed an onslaught of questions and require-ments she hadn't anticipated, most urgently, "How do I keep a human alive when I barely feel alive myself?" Her whole body was aching and changed and raw. Her hormones were raging, and she couldn't recognize herself. At one point she (the most patient, mild-mannered person I've ever encountered) punched a wall! Her son would cry every time she tried to feed him. She wouldn't allow herself to resort to formula because the books and the blogs and every single mother she'd ever met all unanimously insisted, "Breast is best." The only time she ever left the house was to come to set. She'd wrap her baby up in as many layers as she could, trudge through the snow with him, then leave him in an empty trailer with a production assistant she'd just met so that she could go to set, feel useless, and face the death stare from me. She'd never felt more alone in her life either.

By the time the shoot was over the damage was done. After weeks of not talking, we finally made plans to get coffee in her neighborhood one afternoon. Cecilia texted on the day to say the baby had a fever and the nanny had bailed, so she probably wouldn't be able to leave the house. By that point, I knew I'd stopped being her friend and transformed into "the work," so I assumed our plans were canceled and went home without even calling. She didn't say anything at the time, but she was livid that I didn't offer to come over and watch the baby with her. She felt abandoned while I assumed I wasn't welcome.

If I'd been capable of seeing myself as anything other than a victim, things would have been different. If Cecilia had allowed herself to get angry and confront me that day, we wouldn't have lost so much time. Instead, our anger festered. "My biggest regret is that I didn't ask for help. I felt closer to you and our work than my baby. I'd known and loved you for years, while he just showed up and was the cause of so much stress and dread. But I couldn't admit that without feeling like a bad mother. I thought, surely you have to love the baby the moment it claws out of you, right?"

After the show premiered, it was renewed for a second season, but I couldn't agree to it. I was still reeling from my experience of the first. I felt heartbroken and venomous. My dream of having my own TV show had come true, and then transformed into one of those fever dreams where you're running for your life, and you've forgotten all your lines, and also you're naked. Literally. After I said no to season two, my visa was revoked, and I had no choice but to return to New York. The loss of London, the show, and Cecilia compounded and knocked me flat on my back.

But there was still a small glimmer of hope.

Years earlier, our editor Sara had introduced me to an Iranian musician named Kourosh Yaghmaei, whose music evoked images of a film every time I listened to it—specifically scenes of the prerevolutionary Iran from my parents' wedding album. I promised myself that one day I'd make the film to match that soundtrack. As our lives drifted apart after *The Bisexual*, Cecilia decided it was finally time to make that film. All we had were disjointed pieces we'd yet to fit into a larger puzzle: the Kourosh Yaghmaei record, photos of my parents' wedding on the eve of the revolution, and the knowledge of their escape a little over a year later. We didn't know what story we were telling, but each of those elements felt like gold.

By the time we sat down to write it, I'd lost my voice. I didn't trust my instincts anymore. So we put our pens down and tried listening instead. We asked my family the questions I'd always been dying to have answered but had never had the audacity to bring up. It became our job to make sense of all the events that predated me and redirected the course of my life. And as we did this, the craziest thing happened: I gained compassion for my parents and gratitude for the home I'd grown up in. And, slowly, through researching the grief that predated me, I began to meet myself on the other side of all my own grief.

Over the course of five years and five page-one rewrites, Cecilia and I molded every bit of information we could glean about the past into a screenplay. We mostly wrote and rewrote separately, emailing drafts back and forth. We sometimes flew to meet each other in person and overanalyze each detail until the whole thing turned to mush. We discussed walking away from the film so many times I lost count. We attacked it from every possible perspective until we found one that made sense, and it wasn't until after we'd finished the script that we realized we'd written the story of us: two friends torn apart when their lives take them in different directions. The writing of it brought us back to each other.

There's an intensity to close female friendships—the kind where the boundaries blur and it becomes impossible to tell where one of you ends and the other begins. That kind of love is always laced with the tiniest bit of hatred. As long as we were creative partners and trucking along at the same pace, I'd never felt it, but the moment she pulled ahead, I went insane with jealousy. Writing the script together helped me extricate myself from that competition. Still, even now, the small, grimy residue of my jealousy remains. I think it will until I either have children of my own or give up the dream of them.

It's hard to describe what it is to have a soulmate. It's a love that, almost twenty years in, contains the same giddiness as when we first met. I love her family because they made her. I love her husband because she chose him and I can see him through her eyes. I love her kids (there are two now) because they came from her, and I can see her in their eyes. If there was ever anywhere in the world I would choose to be, it's by her side. Even when I can't stand her. Even when I wanted her off my set.

Sometimes we don't speak for weeks. Sometimes it feels like a limb is missing. But I carry her with me. She's still the love of my life, and through all of this I never doubted we'd find our way back to each other, I just didn't know how or when. It's a privilege to have the kind of friendship you can watch morph through the decades. I dream of us in our sixties, kids grown, writing in Italy, shooting in Greece, allowing ourselves more confidence, fewer apologies, and the wisdom to voice our resentments and zap them dead the moment they materialize. She's right, she's still the same person she was before becoming a mother, but somehow I'm not.

Cecilia in the editing room, having it all

You Win Sundance

You win Sundance with your second film. You weren't expecting it. You've never been the winner of anything, not even raffles. Flowers arrive at your door, so many bouquets you run out of receptacles to put them in. It's so shocking that it doesn't feel like real life, but rather something you saw on TV once. It *is* something you saw on TV once because you weren't actually there to receive the award, since you'd already moved on to the next shoot. Instead you watched from your best friend's couch as Chloë Moretz accepted it on your behalf.

Then Hollywood starts calling like it's that popular girl in high school who felt so impossibly aspirational you never even allowed yourself to jerk off to the idea of her. But here she is, asking if you wanna hang. So you go to LA to check out your options.

If you approach LA like it's another country, you'll be charmed by it. The eyes on you the moment you enter a room, scanning for fame, beauty, or wealth, will feel culturally specific to the place and therefore exotic. Like how every room divides up according to people's IMDb STARmeter ranking. It's the custom here. That and eyelash extensions.

It's bright and warm and optimistic. You wake up with an air of calm patience that's eluded you your whole life. Normally you wake up in a mild state of panic, thinking, "The Obamas have already worked out, I might as well give up." But not in LA, where for some reason you can't stop fantasizing about surfing. You, the kid who gave herself a bloody nose while trying to do a forward roll in the third grade. For some reason, since arriving here, you're full-on Sporty Spice, and all your daydreams involve hoisting your weight up onto a narrow plank of wood and steering it across waves as they flatten, like a spatula gliding frosting over cake.

You want a wardrobe that does the heavy lifting of communicating your whole vibe, so you go shopping. Because you're in California, you find yourself gravitating toward linen tunic dresses, wide-brim straw hats, and bracelets—so many bracelets! They speak to you now. *You're an elegant woman of stature who can carry a statement piece,* says a chunky silver cuff. *I'm the touch of color you can wear without looking like you're in Georgia O'Keeffe cosplay because you're not white,* whispers a slim turquoise bangle. A trio of chains you have to snake around your wrist twice screams, *Don't forget—you're still fuckable!* You buy them all and wear them all so they cover 60 percent of your left forearm and think, *This feels right.*

You shove aside the mounting panic over spending money on nonessentials, rationalizing that these are "investment pieces" and from now on *this* is how the new, easy, Los Angeles you dresses. You *need* to spend this money because fast fashion is killing the planet, so this is for the children and *also* because you're a grown-ass woman. Your closet should be permanent collection, not special exhibit. But most important because you should be dressing for the part you want, not the part you have.

The part you have is broke niche indie filmmaker, while the part you *want* is THE MOST BEAUTIFUL AND POWERFUL WOMAN IN THE ROOM. You get home from the well-curated, high-end vintage boutique and model your investment tunic dresses in front of the mirror, only to discover that the part you are now dressed for is Charles Manson Lost Girl.

You'd blow 80 percent of your paycheck if it meant leaving the house feeling like you're dressed as yourself, but what the fuck does that look like?

Lesbians you think you're on a date with (turns out you're not) explain that you're not just a Capricorn but a Cancer rising. Even more important, you're a Pisces moon. And the fact that you're a Capricorn sun, Cancer rising, with a Pisces moon explains everything about your heart and your brain and your ambition and why you ache. Your signs reveal the truth of you, and the truth is YOU ARE A WALKING OPEN WOUND. None of it was you; all of it was predestined in the stars the minute your mother shat you out. Congratulations. Now you're equipped with this knowledge that rings deeply true and changes absolutely nothing. But you're happy to know it, because astrology as therapy is the culture here, and you're enjoying the appropriation, like when you were seventeen and ate a diet of mostly sōmen noodles the year after you did that homestay in Japan.

Hollywood's a lot like high school, only everyone's a theater nerd. The jock, the painfully competitive valedictorian, the homecoming queen: all of them are theater nerds. Extroverted introverts who get off on the performance and the eyes on them. You know this because: it you. The first time you made your parents laugh, like *really* laugh, you were ten, had a scarf wrapped around your hair hijab-style, and said, "Look, Iranian porn!" Then you ripped off the scarf to expose your hair. It took maybe five seconds for their faces to flip from discomfort to laughter, and from that moment you were hooked.

You take meetings, an avalanche of meetings: back-to-back, like speed dating, only each one lasts ninety minutes. Everyone walks in mid-laugh, with glass-half-full smiles and eager eyes. You have to adjust for inflation because when they say they're die-hard fans who think you're a visionary and they'd like to erect a statue in your honor, that means they watched the trailer. It's the Hollywood equivalent of "Nice jacket."

You sit across from a big-shot executive to see if you're a match to direct one of his movies. He's a big man with a hearty laugh and wide-crossed legs. He pitches his slate with an animated and slightly infantile affect, like it's a bedtime story and he's angling for full custody. He's all hands and arms and eyebrows, acting out the plot, beat by beat, with a level of dramatic commitment that betrays he thinks he'd do better as the star and the writer and the director but he chooses not to because those are details and he's all about the big picture, the big money, and the big power.

In a few years the billboard will be on Sunset, but right now the role of *Sullen Teenage Girl Who Just Wants to Breakdance, but Her Conservative Muslim Family Doesn't Approve* is being acted out before your eyes by this dude: the head of the fifth-biggest studio, and the man responsible for rebooting that teen monster borderline snuff franchise you couldn't escape twelve years ago. He's super into transcendental meditation, commutes from his oceanfront property in Santa Monica, and runs ten miles by 7 A.M. Every waiter at this members-only club knows him by name, and the place looks like an exact replica of the Barbie Dream House you fantasized about owning as a girl. The film he's pitching is based on the book, which was based on the podcast, which was based on the fortune cookie he got once at Mr. Chow. Your first lesson in Hollywood is that everyone is thirsty for that sweet, sweet IP, that intellectual property, that built-in audience.

Now he's pitching you his company's whole deal, their brand, their ethos, and as he speaks, the words begin to float away and out of grasp. "We're all about strong female voices with edge that—" Your head nods, but your mind is on the washable silk pajama set you saw online. If you wear it most nights for the next four years, it'll definitely be worth the $278 price tag. Imagine how chic and elegant and comfortable in your skin you'll feel prancing around the apartment, or the hotel room, or the Taylor Swift sleepover you'll be invited to once you're the next woman nominated for best director and—oh wow, this guy is still talking. "—Even though I'm, as you can see, a straight white man (nobody's perfect, haha), I'm reading this script and REALLY relating on a personal level to this girl, because, while I'm not Muslim, and I'm not a breakdancer, I've definitely felt that divide between me and my dad where—"

You wonder if this guy wants to fuck you.

He seems a bit flirty, like he's trying to impress, but that might just be his meeting technique.

Does he know you're not actually here?

Is *he* here?

When you try to engage with what he's saying, you don't get the sense that *he's* engaged. It's more like his face is doing an impression of a face that's engaged in the meeting.

Does *your* face look like it's engaged in the meeting?

Quick, what's the face of a human engaged in the meeting?

When it's your turn to speak, you find yourself falling into the role of "Queer Iranian Female Director" with the joke-to-story ratio of an open mic night. If you agree to work with this man, it'll be his party, and you'll have no real creative power. You'll be the cardboard cutout they hired to pose with.

You shouldn't have taken this meeting.

Wait, no, it's good you're here. This film would pay off all your student debt, and more people would watch it than all the work you've made combined. Quick, start trying to get the job. He needs a Middle Eastern woman with a few features under her belt or he'll look racist, and there are only, like, three of us.

Wait, no, don't take the job. If you saw the trailer for this film, you wouldn't feel compelled to watch it—even if it were on Netflix and you needed something to put on while doing the dishes. Someone who wants to watch this film should make it. You don't do this work because you enjoy deciding where the camera goes and where the people stand; you do it because you have something to say.

Yeah, sure, but who cares what you have to say if nobody's watching? You're too fucking niche. How masturbatory is it to bring more work into an oversaturated marketplace because it speaks to you and, like, three nineteen-year-old lesbians? Maybe you NEED this guy and his stupid commercial concept so you can sneak your voice into the mainstream the way *Wishbone* snuck an English lit lesson into each adventure!

But what if you're legit bad at it? When this bombs, you'll get the blame, not this dude. He'll have at least eight other movies going, and one of them is bound to justify his existence and pay for him to cryogenically freeze his head or whatever the fuck he spends his millions on.

The meetings make you see the work through a new lens of pessimism. Each one chips away at why you do this and why you love it until it's Tetris and you have to fit all the pieces together to try to come up with a movie that is all of the things: Inoffensive, Timely, Profitable, Appealing to Everyone, and Good by all standards of Good versus Bad.

But being liked by all the people was never in your wheelhouse. Not fitting in was what brought you to movies in the first place.

The thing about winning Sundance is that it gives you a sense of entitlement that shifts your goals. You stop being satisfied by just making the films you want to make; now you want to make HISTORY. You want all the eyes. Your ambition is spectacular and crippling. How much audience is enough to justify a film? A TV show? Your life?

It feels like your instincts are betraying you. Now, with each line you write, you begin to imagine who it'll alienate; you hear the criticism and spot the demographics that you left out. So you delete the line and start over, but the next line is no good either. Or the next. The work was how you built your confidence. What do you do now that the work is tearing it down?

Sometimes you get these days, these weeks, these months where it feels impossible to

get

out

of

the fucking

bed.

Why would you? It's so much easier to just stay and hide and rest and enjoy the simple pleasure of not being seen and not even trying.

You start thinking about killing yourself—all the time—not like you're planning, but more like a fantasy permeating all your thoughts. Score playing under dialogue, subtle but persistent, and a bit terrifying. When visiting family in New York, you stand at the top of the Guggenheim and think, *What an elegant platform they've provided for jumping to your death.*

Fuck, it would be so sweet to not have to live anymore.

Alive, you're marinating in a cesspool of shame and anger and guilt that form the kind of pain that throbs. And then there's the rejection—so much rejection you're choking on it. You're choking, but you're also laughing because the fact that you had your own TV show but it didn't get nominated for a BAFTA and now you want to kill yourself is so pathetic it makes you want to kick your own ass.

But you're too old to kill yourself, and you're too old to start cutting again; you're just old enough to know that your thoughts are not facts and what goes down must go up. You know the crazy is renting space in your brain, and it's your job to make that space inhospitable with therapy and meditation and routine and exercise and all of the water and none of the alcohol and trying and trying and trying so hard.

Who knows, maybe this is the "you" you've been waiting to be. A string of acute heartbreaks wipes you clean of partners, both professional and romantic, and you discover the life you were actually "meant" to have, *Under the Tuscan Sun*–style. People say you need a hobby. They tell you there needs to be something in your life that brings you joy outside of work. But you've been alive for a while now. If there was anything else that was capable of bringing you joy, wouldn't you have found it by now? Maybe you quit film and find pottery? Jujitsu? Maybe your worst fears are realized, and you become a bitter film teacher who makes a stand-up routine out of tearing apart student shorts?

But right now you're in LA.

A friend tells you to meet her at something called No Lights, No Lycra. You don't know what it is, but you go without googling because you're giving yourself up to this city and its belief in exercise as a fun social thing to do together on a Thursday night. You arrive at a large empty space that feels like an abandoned warehouse: white walls and high ceilings. You step in and the room goes pitch-black. Your eyes struggle to adjust as your friend's voice appears in one ear.

"You know the deal, right? Solo dance for one hour. No touching, no talking."

And then there's music.

You've had to dance on-screen twice, both under your own direction, and both times you blew it. You found yourself hardening, incapable of melting into the beat. You kept searching for your instincts, but your body couldn't hear them. You just wanted footage of you dancing like yourself: loose, easy, and in sync with the music. Heavy with the hips and Persian with the arms. But both times you were too aware of being seen, and at first this feels like that, like a middle school dance where you forget how to move. But then the chorus kicks in. So your hips kick in. You start to feel it in your shoulders—they get seduced into the beat. You're flirting with yourself. And as you dance, you hear the crazy stirring inside you:

Is this worth doing if nobody's watching?

Which one of us is doing the BEST dancing? There should be a winner.

And if there is a winner, it has to be me.

If it's not me, how pathetic is it that I'm not even the best dancer in this room of theater nerds dancing in the dark?

If it *is* me, then does this even matter? There are so few people here.

This would never exist at home because it's so sincere: people dancing together with all their heart like nobody's watching because nobody is watching and we all Venmo-ed seven dollars to set aside the time and the space to do it.

You've been so removed from your body these past few years. Actually, longer—all of your years. Living in a city like New York or London makes you feel like you're a brain floating above a body, and the body's this annoying drunk friend you have to drag with you everywhere, all "Sorry about her." So you force yourself to take her to the gym or a yoga class, but when you do, it's getting in the way of answering the questions that echo in your head and drive your existence: How am I progressing? What am I making? Where am I succeeding?

But right now in the dark, the volume on the questions lowers. They're there, but the dancing feels like an answer. Here, your brain is sewn to your body, and they work in tandem. You realize you've never danced sober. Not hard, not for an hour straight without a decent buzz and someone you were trying to impress.

You did it for love. Every script, film, interview, conference call. You did it to connect, to be seen, because you felt so invisible and there was so much to say. But now you've been seen, and it's terrifying. You've been seen, but it wasn't enough, and no matter how many wins you get, they'll never satiate, because you keep changing the benchmark of "enough" so that it's just out of reach. So the story always reads that you're a loser and nobody likes you. And now you broke yourself, because you don't know how to stop stripping the meat off your existence so you could inject it onto the screen to make the work more lifelike, leaving your actual life limp and inanimate.

But there's nothing you can do about that just now. So you keep dancing.

This is nice. Dancing without an audience. Dancing without performing. So much of your time is spent performing. It's exhausting. Without an audience, you could do anything.

You dance like you're a stripper, dance like a cyborg. You take up space, you rain sweat, you scrunch up small, jump in place, punch the air, shoot the energy from your groin out your fingertips. And, yeah, okay, you're broken, but deep in your gut you know it's a privilege to be alive. You don't know *why* it is, but you know that it is.

And in the dark, with no eyes on you, you dance the best you've ever danced.

Things That Are Happy (Reasons Not to Kill Yourself)

- Small children wearing prescription glasses.
- The way the sun pours into the living room in the afternoon, no matter what living room you're in.
- Watching a dog have a dream.
- The smell of your mother's sweaters, still holding her perfume, perfectly folded in the drawer.
- The time you almost missed your flight, but the Delta check-in guy rushed you through security, even though he didn't really have to, and smiled as he wished you a good flight home. How it made you feel like you had a home to go home to.
- That feeling you get when wearing the clothes of someone you love—how it can make you feel more like yourself than anything you've ever bought.
- That everything changes. Even when you don't want it to. Even when it feels like it never could.

Newly Single

I'm newly single, newly in my midthirties, newly back in New York, and the thought of romantic love makes me want to projectile-vomit. Dating used to feel like a choose-your-own-adventure. I loved the excitement of discovering what lay behind doors one, two, and three. But now I've opened all the doors, played out all the possibilities, and they were all a bit . . . meh.

It feels like I'm always *just* out of a relationship. It feels like I've single-handedly made "just out of a relationship" my brand. I fall in love so hard, so fast, and every time I'm convinced I've discovered the right formula, the *final* formula, but then the formula malfunctions and I'm back where I started, heartbroken and licking my wounds.

It's too easy to fall in love. You just open your eyes to someone's greatness and open yourself up to being seen. And even though I can always spot it from a mile away, it never feels like I have a choice in the matter. I have no self-control—I'm the kind of reader who jumps to page 300 to see who did it; when

I get takeaway, a third of the food's gone before I've even entered the house. I fall in love without fully knowing a person, and by the time I realize we're incompatible it's too late—we've got Christmas plans and baby names. I'll spend the next twelve to fifteen months talking myself into staying until eventually one of our lives will hit a crisis, and it'll unravel the whole relationship. The loving is easy; it's knowing which differences are benign and which are fatal that's the hard part.

Everyone I've loved lived up to my first impression of them. It wasn't just lust or a projection or desperation. I fell for the sliver I saw in those first moments. It would be easier if I could say I'd been delusional, but I can't. I've lost great people, and on some level I'm still a bit in love with all six of them. Six! Six names I wrote down as emergency contacts and walked through Immigration with and told the story of my nose job. One taught me how to ski, another to love marmite, and another to rinse out the recycling. I miss one's logic, one's hands, one's family, and the nook of one's armpit, which is where I slept the best sleep of my life. I continue finding new great qualities in new great partners, but I'm never able to replace what's left behind.

After each breakup I promise myself that next time will be different. Like a pendulum, I swing from one set of irreconcilable differences to another: I love too much, they love too much. They're too different from me, then they're too similar to me. It feels like I've tried every type of person, and I haven't found the type that works. *Is* there a type that works?

My last person possessed the kind of disarming warmth and beauty that made him seem like he was from another dimension: David Bowie face, long lean limbs, low velvet voice, and the patient adoration of your mother on a good day. The courtship was too perfect, too seemingly scripted for the chick lit demographic with me as a Middle Eastern Bridget Jones: brash, messy thirty-something who almost always says the wrong thing gets swept off her feet by Prince Eric–style dream boy. I kinda knew it wasn't right when we were eating noodles and he latched on to one of mine until we were kissing. He did it like he'd single-handedly invented sharing a noodle and parlaying it into a kiss in that exact moment. Like *Lady and the Tramp* never happened. Something in me said, *This isn't going to last, is it?* In the end it always adds up to the same thing: your crazy doesn't fit mine. Nobody did a 180, it just wasn't right. Game over, try again.

Now I'm back in New York and determined to sell this move as a choice I've made, instead of the truth, which is that my visa was revoked. Star (my ex-girlfriend, two girlfriends ago) is falling in love. She looks happy and hopeful and renewed. When I meet her new person, I'm grateful to see that she's found something so much stronger than we ever could have been. I ask Star, "What do I do about the loneliness?"

"You turn it into solitude."

She's right. I have to learn how to turn this loneliness into solitude. I rent a one-bedroom in Boerum Hill. I say yes to every invitation. I reach out to people I haven't spoken to in years and cook them dinner before I even have furniture to serve it on.

It turns out solitude blows. The neighbor across the street from my new apartment throws these big, loud dinner parties with fairy lights that fill me with the kind of envy that increases your heart rate. I hate them. Their music sucks, one of them laughs like a hyena, and I would do absolutely anything to join them. That hyena laugh keeps interrupting the YouTube clips of *Say Yes to the Dress* that I play back-to-back on my phone as I carry it around the apartment like I'm the world's saddest incarnation of Radio Raheem. If this were a movie, my character would write a short note, tape it to a remote-control airplane, and fly it over to the party roof. Then, by the time I flew the plane back, there'd be a new note for me.

I have to stop doing this. I'm like James Stewart in *Rear Window*, only instead of seeing murders, I see romantic comedy "meet-cutes."

I'm losing track of all the people I've been in love with, losing the labels on the memories I've filed away. One of my exes used to fill their mouth with big gulps of water and then stream it into my mouth bird-style when I was too lazy to move after sex. The water from her mouth (was it a her?) to my lips would melt into wide wet kisses. I loved it. Until I didn't. Who did I do that with? I remember the water and the skin and the tongue, but not the face.

"Hey, I saw you doing your thing in there. You deserve more love than you have right now."

A man tells me this outside a nightclub at around four in the morning, and I can't tell if it's a come-on or a drive-by shooting. How does he know that I don't have love? Could he smell it on me? His smile is friendly, without an agenda. We've both been dancing for hours. Lately I've developed an appreciation for techno and house and neon and club drugs. I like it loud and anonymous when the music and your limbs start communicating with each other and your brain shuts the fuck up, and for a few precious moments all you feel is warmth: for your body and the other bodies and the wordless exchange between them as we share the same heartbeat.

I came to the club with friends, but they left early, and when they left I made myself stay because I didn't want to be the type of girl who can't stay out on her own because I am cool, goddammit, and a grown-ass woman, and I can stay out as long as I damn well please! So I danced by myself, head down, feeling more self-conscious than I did in sixth grade, changing into my gym clothes by layering them on top of my school clothes in an inverse *Flashdance*.

"You deserve more love than you have right now."

Is this guy expressing sympathy, or is he volunteering for the job? I feel like I'm maybe supposed to *thank* him? Is that right? But when I turn to say something, he's disappeared.

I meet a guy through friends of friends. He's strange in this way that makes me feel compelled to know more before deciding if it's sexy or insufferable. It seems like he's intrigued by me but not necessarily attracted to me—more like he thinks I should make a movie based on his life? I'm so desperate to have a thing to do each night that I might just offer to. We hang out low-key: music videos and weed in his apartment late one night. He tells me about the twenty-year-old he's sleeping with. He says that he asked her to reveal her deepest sexual fantasy so he could fulfill it, and *she* said it was a threesome with two dudes, but no gay shit. And this guy, being the sexually adventurous saint he is, made her wish come true. I'm not sure why straight men feel compelled to talk to me like this: friend-zoning and dick-measuring and negging all at once.

I think about that poor girl, so desperate to impress this man over twice her age that she lies through her teeth so he'll think her deepest desire just happens to be offering up the opportunity for him to reach his lifelong goal of double penetration with his bff. He drops the sticky details onto my lap like it's a challenge. It doesn't feel like an invitation; it feels like I'm back in high school when Jake Brown pushed me onto the ground, straddled me, and gave me a play-by-play of how he lost his virginity.

If this were a few years ago, I'm pretty sure this dude would be inside me within the next thirty minutes. But because I'm not distracted by my usual goal of tricking him into bed, I have the space to get a sense of his personality. I'm not crazy about it. He's the kind of guy who likes to teach you things, like theories that Covid was caused by 5G. There's a reason he's fucking a girl more than twenty years his junior, and it's not just because she's "so mature for her age."

I know exactly what it would be like to fuck this guy: athletic, playful, and a little performative because he seems a bit theatrical. I'd be holding in my stomach the whole time, and he'd lose interest the second he came. Ten minutes after that, I'd be on my hands and knees, digging in the crevices of his ancient velour couch, where I'd most likely find two corroded AA batteries before locating my bra.

I'd be cognizant of my crusty underwear the whole ride home, and the next day I'd alternate between feeling like a badass and an idiot as the graphic visuals of the messier moments of the evening would surface like snapshots. He'd text something nice but vague and noncommittal around 4 P.M. two days later. We'd see each other for stoned sex in five days, no dinner. It would continue like that for about a month, at which point he'd flake and it would be my undoing because of the way that getting touched can become addictive. He wouldn't notice the difference because he has two or three girls in rotation and a really elaborate gaming setup that seems to have taken the place of human love.

But it's not a few years ago, so I don't make a move. Instead, I nod and "Uh huh" in agreement and ask follow-up questions so he knows I'm cool. I wonder if he's thinking the same thing I am: *Why am I here if we're not fucking?* The thought of watching the sun rise in this guy's apartment with all my clothes on is too depressing, so I get up to leave. We're both all smiles and "Let's do this again sometime," but of course we never do.

I can't date anymore. There's this new voice in my head—the voice of a woman who has been there and done that. Shit. I'm going to die your weird aunt who isn't actually your aunt, buys all her jewelry at MoMA, and shows up on Christmas Day with educational toys and a fruit tart.

I usually get over a person by getting under ten. Single and celibate is uncharted territory. What do I do now? Peaches was wrong, you can't "fuck the pain away"—not really. You can only kick it out of sight for a bit. Perhaps I've been kicking it down the road for nineteen years, jumping from one codependent relationship to the next with brief slutty interludes acting as palate cleansers in between.

My last girlfriend said her dog (the one that used to be *our* dog) has calmed down a lot since she's been spayed. Will I find calm on par with my ex-dog now that I've stopped humping all the legs? I think about what Star said and consider what solitude might look like. It's strange having to face myself without the distraction of sex and attention and flirting at parties. Now that I spend so much time alone, I'm becoming more cognizant of the dialogue I'm having with myself all day, every day, and it sounds a lot like schoolyard bullying. What did I do to earn my own disdain? I was eleven years old when my request to take part in Clueless: The Recess Game was rejected, and it became clear that perhaps I should start hating myself. I remember *realizing* I wasn't good enough, but I don't remember *why* I wasn't good enough. I still can't figure that one out.

"You turn it into solitude."

All these years, I've been hoping I could find the person who'd love me so much I could scoop up the overflow and see myself through their eyes, but it turns out that kind of love is nontransferable. What are the rules for loving yourself? The technique? I'm not sure what it would even look like. It's gotta mean something that I've been spending my days half-watching *Say Yes to the Dress*, a show where women try on gowns that cost four times their rent until they've found the one that transforms them into what they think is the most lovable version of themselves. They're not just dresses, they're costumes, and it's not just a wedding, but a play the bride writes, directs, and stars in as The Girl Who Is Loved. She gathers everyone she knows to witness her and her partner promise to DIE in their relationship. I'd like to learn how to enjoy my relationship with myself, as it's definitely the relationship I'm going to die in.

I think I might be done looking for a love that'll heal me. I'll have to face all my shame without the aid of a distraction. Maybe if I took the time to really face and examine it, I'd see that I'm killing myself over shit I'd never hold against someone else. I mean, some of it I *would* hold against someone else, but perhaps, eventually, I could learn to ease up on that too. I bet if I did, I could open my eyes to what I love about myself. Then maybe, who knows, I could turn to a relationship to fulfill *other* needs—needs that would have nothing to do with validating my existence. Like someone to laugh at all my stupid *L Word* jokes. I bet that would be pretty great.

Should I Make a Human
or a Movie?

Malibu is seductive. It'll lure you out of your unathletic indoor-kid nature and into the water, which is bluer than any you've seen in real life. It's calm and shabby chic and makes you think you 100 percent cannot die without figuring out how to buy a home on the beach. Why have you never lived near a beach? Sitting in an Adirondack chair and watching the waves crash would be so much more effective than that $300 weighted blanket you hoped might magically fix your personality flaws. The waves would comfort you. They'd calm your racing heart. They'd remind you you're such a small part of the earth's much bigger story.

Everything in Malibu is muted and tasteful, and the houses are incongruous in a funny way that tells you everything you need to know about each individual homeowner. Sometimes, if you're lucky, you'll meet one of those homeowners stepping out of their doors and onto the sand to run along the beach with their golden retrievers. Nine times out of ten they're retired and used to work in the music industry. They'll volunteer their whole life story and the story of every house on the beach if you just keep smiling.

But I'm not on the beach. I'm bedbound and have been repeatedly told that under no circumstances am I to run or stretch or engage in any kind of exercise or else my ovaries might flip. I just underwent an egg retrieval, which is when your eggs are extracted from your ovaries via a needle connected to a suction device and then frozen for future use via IVF. But before the eggs can be extracted, they're pumped up via daily hormone injections.

After the procedure I woke up feeling calm and giddy with relief that after weeks of meticulous measuring and stomach stabbing and waiting-room waiting there was nothing left for me to do but lie still and try to forget about the small fortune I'd just dropped for the privilege of putting my body through this. This Malibu trip is my attempt at recuperating in style. My girlfriend booked it because she's the type of person who can go for a hike at 4 P.M. on a Tuesday and read for pleasure and travel for the sake of exploration instead of film promotional purposes. She has an innate talent for transforming the half-empty into the half-full, and that's why we're in one of those weirdly fancy motels off the Pacific Coast Highway that looks like it was remodeled by new owners exactly three years ago, based on the hand-dyed kimonos, terrazzo tiles, and strategic use of millennial pink. There isn't a cloud in the sky. It's offseason, so the beach feels like it's your very own, but I'm not faring as well as I'd hoped. Last week I'd pictured myself writhing all sexy in the sand like Madonna in the "Cherish" video, but instead I'm writhing in bed because it feels like I'm being repeatedly kicked in the stomach while spinning in the rinse cycle.

The worst of it isn't the pain; it's the uncertainty. I won't know for days whether they extracted any eggs that are mature enough to freeze. If they did extract eggs that are healthy enough to freeze, there's no guarantee that any of them will be viable once they're unfrozen. And if they *are* viable once they're unfrozen, not all of them are likely to become embryos when I'm finally able to lock down some sperm. And if, by some miracle, I wind up with a healthy embryo, it's not a given that it'll implant successfully or that I'll carry the pregnancy to term. I hadn't quite understood this sequence of "ifs" when I began this process. I have about a 35 percent chance of success. I went into this thinking I could buy peace of mind. Now I'm shocked at my naivete.

I did it impulsively. My friend Rowan had been trying to convince me to get my eggs frozen for years, and every time the subject came up I'd declare, conclusively, that egg freezing was a no-go. I figured if I wasn't able to get pregnant it would be the universe's way of telling me to adopt, but I'd always had this gut feeling it wouldn't be hard for me to get pregnant. The general feedback I'd received from immigrant grandmothers of all races was that I had childbearing hips, and on those grounds alone I felt I was owed fertility. There had to be a benefit to this girth. So I spent my youth weirdly confident that motherhood was my fate and that it would come naturally when the time was right. The concept of using artificial reproductive technologies to build a family felt intrinsically icky. Why should I play God and decide that I was above nature? "No judgment," I'd tell people. "But it's not right for *me*."

But then Rowan gave birth to her son, Reza, and the moment I saw him, perfect and Persian and so hairy his ears were coated in fur, all my arguments against medical intervention disintegrated. He wasn't a test-tube baby, he was just a baby— *her* baby. I looked at him and thought, *How did we ever exist without him here, in her arms?* Suddenly none of the details of how he was conceived mattered—all that mattered was that he was here.

Two weeks later I was having a transvaginal ultrasound, and the day after that, $3,000 worth of injectable hormones arrived at my door with absolutely no instructions at all.

The thing I couldn't have anticipated when I made those anti-intervention proclamations was how desperate I'd be for proximity to my heritage. I want my child to share my culture and my country and my original nose, and I know that I could share at least some of these things with a child of any race, but I'm scared that my connection to my own is dying. I'm scared my family's grip on our identity is slipping, and soon it'll end with me. In fact, for the first time in twenty years, I miss my old nose. I want evidence of my ethnicity on my face, and I'm jealous of my brother for escaping adolescence with his intact.

I'm scared I'd fail a child of a different ethnicity. How could I speak with any authority on what it is to be anything other than Iranian in America? So much of my life has been a wrestling match with identity, and I don't want to put another person in that position if I can avoid it. It's also why I'm freezing eggs instead of embryos. The doctor, my family, and my friends all suggested I just go to a sperm bank and buy some sperm. Freezing an embryo has a far higher rate of success than freezing an egg, but I want the sperm to come from someone my kid will know and love—who is preferably Iranian.* I'm beginning to think that the previous gut feeling wasn't a prophecy but a refusal to even consider the fact that I might end up with a woman or alone.

I hate that my girlfriend can't impregnate me. She's the person I want to raise a child with, and the fact that we can't create

---

*And hot, so they don't get voted the ugliest person at their school.

one that's half her and half me makes this whole pursuit feel ridiculous, like we're playacting at family. I know that's not true, but it's how it feels when it's 3 A.M. and the California Cryobank just sold out of the guy you thought could *maybe* be the biological father of your child because his handwriting was the most legible and he said he likes swimming. From the moment the first hormone injection entered me, every cell in my body screamed in protest: *THIS ISN'T RIGHT, YOU SHOULDN'T BE DOING THIS!* I was convinced I could actually *feel* it working its way inside me, and it felt like poison. It felt like punishment for being gay.

Nobody at the fertility clinic told me much about the hormones before they'd arrived at my door—neither how to inject them nor what dosage to inject. I just increased my spending limit, handed over my credit card, and hoped for the best. My girlfriend and I had to FaceTime my doctor, who walked us through it on a Friday night while her five-year-old screamed and yanked at her shirtsleeve. Why did I go into this so blind? Maybe if I'd known what I was doing, it could have been a fun wacky experiment? I should've asked more questions when I was with the nurse, I should've taken notes, and the fact that I failed to go into this first small step toward parenthood prepared makes me wonder how the hell I could ever manage to pull off being a mother.

"Being a mother is fucking painful. It is paaaaaaaainful. Don't do it. No matter what, you get the blame. If the kid doesn't blame you, you blame yourself." This is what my old boss Laura told me. "I, for one, would love to see a little Desiree running around in the world" is what three friends who do not have children, but would like to have children, have each said to me on separate occasions. When I ask Cecilia what I should do, she says that she can't tell me but that she envies women who aren't interested in having kids. My mother says,

"I will raise your child for you." And I know that now that she's older, she'd be different: calm and patient and fun and present and all the things a parent should be. But would I?

I always knew I wanted to be a mother, the way I always knew I didn't want to be buried alive, the way I knew I wanted to be beautiful and successful, with huge, gravity-defying tits. When I was growing up, adults without kids seemed tragic. Or at least that's how my parents talked about them, like their lives couldn't possibly be worth living without the gift of constant caretaking. But I'm not sure I'm capable of that kind of focused, all-in devotion. How could I be when there hasn't been a moment of my adult life when I wasn't desperately trying to nurture a film into existence? How could a child compete? I know a mother can become a filmmaker, but should a filmmaker become a mother?

It's now or never. Even if fertility weren't an issue, I'm watching myself grow more rigid with each passing year. I like things the way I like them: surfaces cleared, clothes folded. I bristle at loud noises, I take long baths, I get overwhelmed by crowds, I feel like my whole body's being twisted up into a giant knot if I don't have enough uninterrupted time to myself by the end of the day. It feels like motherhood's a young woman's game. But I was a baby when I was a young woman. Cecilia got pregnant when we were thirty-three, and it felt way too early for kids. Five years passed in the blink of an eye. Now I'm thirty-eight and at the end of the road. How did I slide so quickly from too young to too old? Where was the sweet spot?

I'm currently using a Hitachi magic wand for its intended purpose of massaging my neck and not my crotch. I believe this is the universal gay lady sign that it's time to take me out back and put me out of my misery. My back was out for the majority of last month. I couldn't even *hold* a baby, let alone carry one inside me, but still, I crave one with everything I've got. I crave one exactly like I craved each film.

Cecilia's right: I envy the women who don't want this. I wish I were above the need to have children. It feels basic, like how I wanted a Kate Spade bag in seventh grade because everyone at school had one. Is becoming a mother the adult equivalent of carrying a Kate Spade bag at Horace Mann High School circa 1998? The best choices in my life have been immune to the desperation to be like others, but the pressure's started up again. I don't know when the road divided, but it has, and now I'm paused at the fork. Which do you wanna be: A mother or a free woman? The good daughter or the workaholic? Lately, I lie in bed and cull through the memories of the day, the week, the month, the year, and I wonder: What happened that I can ascribe my shame to tonight? But nothing actually happened—I just watched another day pass without moving any closer to motherhood.

"It's your age," Rowan tells me. "I was scared too at thirty-eight—neither old nor young. The biological clock gets loud and then one day it'll halt, but you don't know when, and it won't take batteries." I hate that it's called a biological clock when it feels more like a screaming kettle—like you left the house with the stove on and your keys in the door. It feels like you dove too deep and are rushing to the surface for air. I dove too deep into my work and my FOMO and my desperate need for validation.

Do I have it in me to make someone else's life worth living when I've had so many doubts about my own? I wish you could test-drive the job before you go ahead and commit to it. What if I'm spectacularly bad at it? An entire life would suck because of me. I can't even care for a dog without going blind with rage over its inability to shit when and where I want it to. If I had a child, my whole existence would revolve around its shit for at least five years, which would be just about time to start worrying about my own incontinence.

The truth of motherhood feels like it's shrouded in mystery. Sometimes I wonder if the joy and horror of it are so great that all mothers have made a silent pact to keep it vague. Or perhaps there are no words for it, the way it feels impossible to fully communicate exactly what it's like to be your mother's daughter.

Here are my questions:

- Is it painfully boring?
- Do you miss your autonomy on an hourly basis?
- Do you ever regret it? (Be honest.)
- Did it fill the bottomless hole that you kept trying to fill with attention and sex and alcohol and drugs and food and whatever else was within arm's reach?
- Can you still be the kind of all-in obsessive perfectionist workaholic who's often cold and distant when lost in the weeds with whatever crisis needs solving?
- If not, what do you become instead?

Does parenthood transform you into an adult? That would be cool. I thought becoming an adult was being profiled in *The New York Times* and getting four stars in *The Guardian* and locking tongues with the hottest person in the room. I thought it was self-expression and cash to burn and going to the right parties with the best outfit, but I did those things, and I still don't feel like an adult. Is it home ownership, three square meals, and sober nights that end at ten with a good book and a $95 candle? It seems like adulthood can't possibly happen without nurturing something outside your own ego.

Could I be someone's mother all day, every day, for all the days I have left? Last week I fought the strongest impulse to zip up an open backpack hanging off the shoulders of the girl standing in front of me on the train. Can that be submitted as evidence? Some might argue that directing is not unlike being the parent of your set: you have an eye on everything relating to the well-being of your movie, and you spend the duration of production driven by the instinct to throw yourself in front of a bus to protect it. But the thing about filmmaking is that it makes you lose your ability to put other people's needs before the work. It seems like the better you become at making films, the worse you are at being a functional human being.

At thirty-eight you know too much, but you still don't know enough.

Am I just trying to make a friend? Is it *cruel* to create a friend? I mean, the kid wouldn't be my *only* friend. Is it fucked up to admit that right now it feels like I'm missing an arm without the presence of my child? That meeting them and then coexisting alongside them feels like it would be a major component of why I exist? Is it wrong to assume that building a family with a partner would be the ultimate collaborative experience? Maybe there is no logic to wanting a baby. Maybe it doesn't need to make sense. Maybe it's primal, like falling in love. I want it because I want it. It's not fair or right, it just is. When I start to break it down, the logic turns to mush.

"This feels wrong," I told my mother through tears, forty-eight hours into the egg-freezing process. "It feels like I shouldn't be doing this—injecting myself with hormones morning and night is unnatural. Like I'm playing God." I heard her sigh on the other side of the line—not with frustration, but with compassion.

"Desi, my pregnancy with you was unnatural."

At first, I have no idea what she's talking about—I've never considered it from that perspective—but then I realize she's right. When my mother was pregnant with me, she had complications due to a cyst and started having contractions in her fourth month. They put her on an experimental medication to stop her contractions, and she wasn't allowed to move for the rest of her pregnancy. "That drug had never been tested. I was on bed rest for so long that I was covered in sores. If I hadn't taken those unnatural drugs and played God, you wouldn't be here."

The hardest part of being a late bloomer is the patience required. When *Appropriate Behavior* got into Sundance, all I could think was *I wish I could have believed in the inevitability of my success. It would have saved me so much heartache.* Now, a decade later, I would like to give myself that same advice: allow yourself to believe in the inevitability of your family, whatever shape it takes. And in the meantime, enjoy the process: of being unsure, of not knowing if the eggs will be viable, of falling in and then out of love, of discovering what it is you're trying to say by writing six different iterations of what you're *not* trying to say. There's so much joy you keep missing out on because you've got your eye on the prize.

I used to hope that with age and beauty and popularity I might stop embarrassing myself, but those hopes were in vain. I'll always be embarrassing, but I'm beginning to lose my embarrassment. The sharp sting of humiliation grows dull when you realize that you're going to keep making a fool of yourself, because that's what it is to be alive. A friend of mine was tucking in her (extremely neurotic) seven-year-old one night when the little girl asked what the point of life was. My friend said she needed a day to think about it. She spent the next morning scrambling to come up with an answer that wouldn't scar the kid for life, but that afternoon her daughter burst through the door with an air of calm joy that had always eluded her, announcing, "I figured out the point of life!"

"Great! What is it?"

"It's to learn things and have fun!"

It's so simple. We're here to learn things and have fun. You can't learn anything without embarrassing yourself, at least a little bit, and you can't have fun if you let that embarrassment swallow you whole.

Yavash yavash translates into "slowly, slowly" in Farsi. You use it when you're nearing action: "Slowly, slowly, we're going to leave the party," "Slowly, slowly, I'm getting better at reading Farsi," "Slowly, slowly, I'm trying to convince the men in my life that the movie *Sideways* kinda sucks." I wonder if, slowly, slowly, I'm building a family. I'm just not sure what it'll look like or how long it'll take me because there's no template. But my parents had no template for living a life outside Iran. Perhaps the template is something that gets rewritten with each generation. Perhaps I need to let go of my desperation to hold on to my culture and give in to whatever this next rewrite is.

"Fuck 'em if they can't take a joke" is what my father would say if he could hear me, and I think I finally get it. Stop taking everything so seriously. If you want a child, you have to take a leap of faith and say "Fuck it" to the consequences. Fuck 'em if they can't take a joke. Fuck your crippling fears, fuck popularity, fuck likability, fuck fuckability, fuck the shame you inherited and the shame you picked up along the way. Fuck all the things that keep you at arm's length from good and right and normal because good and right and normal weren't built for girls like you. Tell the stories they told you to shut up about, the shit that keeps you up at night, and do it on your own terms. Chase the life your instincts pull you toward, even if your instincts sometimes lead you astray. Trust that they'll take you *somewhere*. And then, once you're there, take the time to bask in the glory of all the space you carved out for yourself and your size 11 feet.

Hopes for
My Forties

- The ability to intuit the right-size Tupperware for the leftovers
- To find a travel outfit that will make me feel like an adult woman instead of a twelve-year-old on a school trip
- To commit to one haircut (and relationship)
- To shed all the shame like an old skin

Acknowledgments

This book wouldn't exist without Caitlin McKenna's patience and brilliance. Thank you for holding my hand as I learned how to be a prose writer. I presented you with nothing but nonsense scribblings for eight years straight, and you helped me weave it into an actual book. Thank you.

Thank you, Emma Caruso, for joining us in the thick of it and guiding me through the toughest patch of the journey.

Thank you, Katie Bowden, for taking me past the finish line.

Thank you, Kim Witherspoon, for convincing me I had a book in me.

I would like to thank my friends for their eyes, ears, notes, and love: Hannah and Emily Almond-Barr, Stacey Berman, Katie Carpenter, Maria Dyer, Will Emsworth, Morgan Evans, Halley Feiffer, Kira Frieje, Cecilia Frugiuele, Jess Greenawalt, Liz Holm, Sophie Hyde, Ingrid Jungermann, Markus Kirschner, Davo McConville, Carmen McLeod, Rowan Riley, Starling Sawyer, Sara Shaw, and Lauren Smitelli.

Hannah Mackay, thank you for your faith—in me, my voice, and this book. I couldn't have found it without you.

Thank you to my family—the Akhavans, Mahallatis, Tabrizians, and Debells—for your support, encouragement, and for accepting me as I am (and allowing me my stories).

Thank you, Yaddo, for the time and space.

Thank you to all the people whose work helped bring this book into being: Rebecca Berlant, Maria Braeckel, Madison Dettlinger, Windy Dorresteyn, Benjamin Dreyer, Elizabeth Eno, Cassie Gonzales, Erica Gonzalez, Ben Greenberg, Michelle Kane, Greg Kubie, Greg Mollica, Rachel Parker, Tom Perry, Alison Rich, Felicity Rubenstein, Noa Shapiro, Robert Siek, Andy Ward, Maria Whalen, and Katie Zilberman.

DESIREE AKHAVAN is a filmmaker and writer. She created the Hulu original series *The Bisexual* and directed the films *Appropriate Behavior* and *The Miseducation of Cameron Post*, which won the Sundance Grand Jury Prize. As an episodic director, she's worked on numerous TV shows, including *Hacks* and *Ramy*. Her writing has appeared in *The Guardian* and *British Vogue*.

ABOUT THE TYPE

This book was set in a Monotype face called Bell. The Englishman John Bell (1745–1831) was responsible for the original cutting of this design. The vocations of Bell were many—bookseller, printer, publisher, typefounder, and journalist, among others. His types were considerably influenced by the delicacy and beauty of the French copperplate engravers. Monotype Bell might also be classified as a delicate and refined rendering of Scotch Roman.